Who Is She?

History and Contributions of the Black Woman from Past to Present

ELOGEIA HADLEY

S.H.E. PUBLISHING, LLC

For information contact: www.shepublishingllc.com

Cover and Title Page Design by Michelle Phillips of CHELLD3 3D VISUALIZATION AND DESIGN

ISBN: 978-1-953163-49-3

Second Edition: February 2024

10 9 8 7 6 5 4 3 2 1

TABLE OF
CONTENTS

ACKNOWLEGMENTS

First, I want to give all praises to the highest God, for giving me the strength to write and inspire. Thank you, Queen Isabella (Faye) and Prophet Lott (Julius), for giving me the ability to think and seek out knowledge for myself. I also want to acknowledge all my family, friends and supporters for believing in my passion for history and putting up with my rants and impromptu history lessons. In addition, I want to recognize the many master teachers from past to present that did the work to tell our TRUE history. I will always be grateful!

ELOGEIA HADLEY

PREFACE

I want you to understand why I wrote it. I asked myself for years, just like many African American people, "Who Am I?" More importantly, who was I as a black woman in this world? For five years, I went on a journey to find out, and this book is the result of much of what I found. Knowing that our contributions have been ignored or over looked, I knew how important it is to "know thyself." This book will give you a glimpse of many of the contributions specifically from black women throughout the African (Black) diaspora. However, Moreover, I start a conversation with black women about who we are and our contributions.

When I wrote this book, I did not want it to be too preachy, but face some realities and debunk some stereotypes about black women in general. As I researched, I found that as black women, we have always been strong mentally, emotionally, and physically. Black women are warriors, survivors, friends, lovers, nurturers, divas, mothers, goddesses, healers, wives, sisters, aunts, confidants and sheroes. However, the world has never seen all the best parts of us.

I hope you find out who you are through this book.

Who is SHE?

WHO IS SHE?

ELOGEIA HADLEY

HER-STORY

African women have not had their stories told throughout history. The accomplishments of African women are not seen as important and these women are, many times, seen as second-class citizens who should be seen and not heard or are supposed to give many the idea women just stood on the sideline and watched history happen and not participate; but to my surprise, black women were at the forefront of it all. Black African women were generals in armies, healers, midwives, warriors and so much more. The black African woman has always been a multifaceted part of history with her contributions and continues to make history to date.

Scientific Eve
" The Eve Gene"

Many scientists believe the African wo-man is the only organism that possesses the Mitochondrial DNA that has all the variations possible for every different human being on Earth. It is called the "Eve Gene." When the genetics of a black woman mutate, she can create any eye color, hair color and skin pigmentation. The darkest African woman can create any type of human being on the planet. No other woman on Earth can do that. There was a time on this planet when all human life was in Africa, and it has been researched that all human life is a descendant of one woman. An African woman!

Lupita Nyongo
Actress

O n the PBS channel "finding Your Roots" traced Lupita's DNA to the oldest maternal Haplogroup that is a direct connection to MT-DNA, known as Mitochondrial "EVE," . Many scientists believe scientific EVE is the mother of all living humans today. Lupita Nyongo's DNA predates race and all other ethnic groups that formed later outside of Africa.

Dinkinesh "Lucy"

Dated to 3.2 million years ago

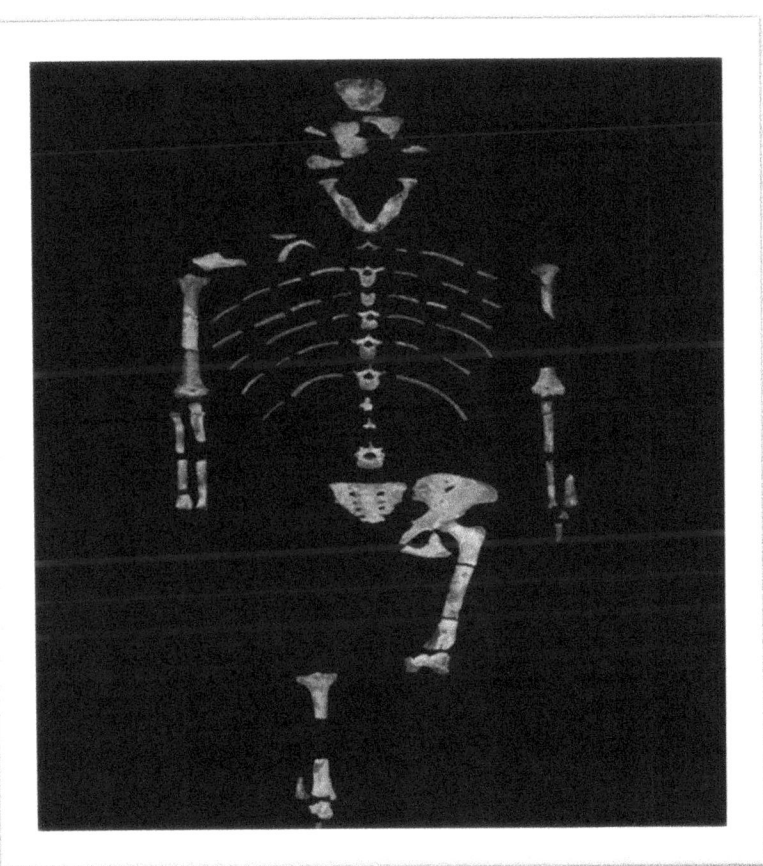

I n 1974, near Hadar Africa in the awash valley, several hundred pieces of bone fossils made up about 40 percent of the skeleton of a female of the hominin species, Australopithecus afarensis. The bones labeled as AL 288-1, named Dinkinesh by the Ethiopians, which means "you are marvelous" and named Lucy by paleoanthropologist Donald Johansson of the Cleveland Museum of Natural History, Yves Coppens and Maurice Taïeb. The Lucy specimen is an early australopithecine dated to 3.2 million years ago.

Luzia

Dated 12,000 years old

Most are taught that African people first arrived in the Americas during the trans-Atlantic slave trade. However, that history is being changed as archaeologists continue to find evidence that Black Africans occupied the Americas before Mongolian Asians crossed the Bering Strait. According to the BBC documentary series' Ancient Voices, the first people were the Black aboriginals of Africa or Australia. It is believed, from the evidence found, that invading Asians later may have entered married or massacred them. From all evidence found, African descendants were the first to populate the land we called the Americas. There were human skulls uncovered in Lagoa Santa, Minas Gerais, Brazil and South America that were dated over 12,000 years old. In 1998, Walter Neves, an archaeologist from the University of Manchester, England did measurements and reconstruction of the oldest skull called Luzia and the measurements showed that Luzia was not mongoloid at all, but he determined the features were of a Negroid. So, Luzia was an African descendent. A black woman!

Queen Nefertiti
(Neferneferuaten)
1370 B.C.

The name is Egyptian and means "the beautiful one has come." It is believed that she lived from around 1370 B.C. Nefertiti was the Great Royal Wife of Akhenaten, an

ELOGEIA HADLEY

Egyptian Pharaoh. Nefertiti and her husband were known for a religious revolution, in which they worshiped one God, Aten, or the sun. She was revered as one of the most beautiful women in the world, however, several parts of her life, including her origins and death remain, a mystery. Many believe Nefertiti may have been from Kush or what is now, Sudan.

Ivory Bangle Lady

4th century AD

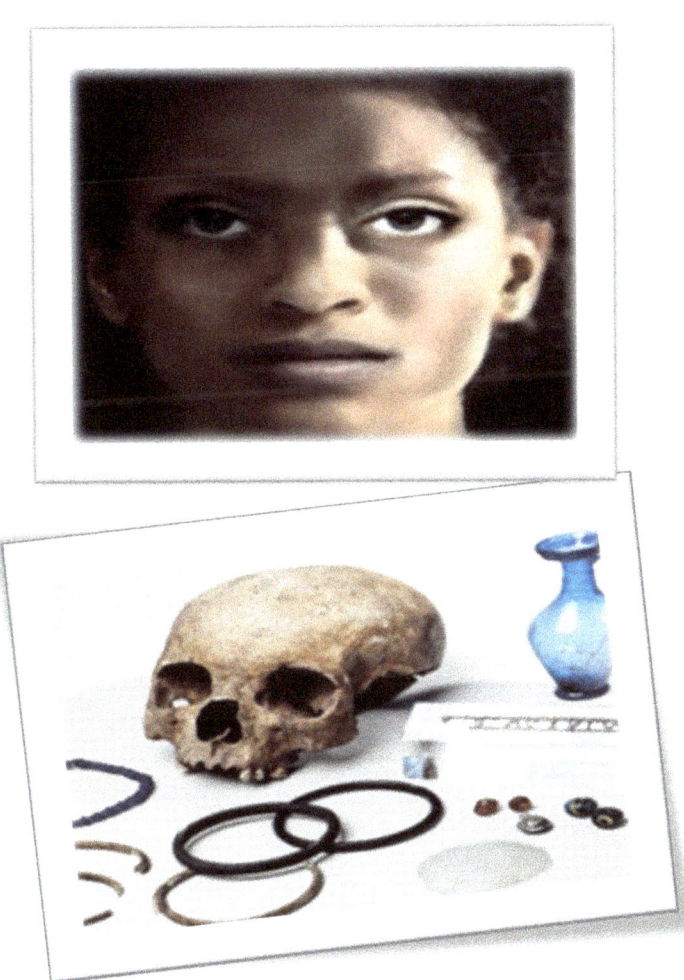

Ivory Bangle Lady was found buried in a stone sarcophagus accidentally found in 1901 by workers in the process of expanding a street near Sycamore Terrace York that is located midway between Bootham and the River Ouse. It was first a mystery until a closer examination of her skeleton has shown that she was a woman of African ancestry and had to be one of the wealthiest inhabitants of fourth-century Roman York. Her stone sarcophagus showed evidence of luxury imports including jewelry made of elephant ivory, a mirror and a blue glass perfume jar, all considered elaborate and expensive at that time. A piece of bone inscribed with the words, "Hail sister may you live in God" was also found with her skeleton.

Queen Shanakhdakheto (Shanakdakhete)

170 to 150 BC

Shanakhdakheto was a Queen (Kandake) of the Kingdom of Kush modern-day Sudan, in Meroë. She is the earliest known ruling

ELOGEIA HADLEY

African Kandake of ancient Nubia, said to have ruled with full power in the Meroë Empire and without a king. She played a significant role in the Meroitic religion and inventing their language. In the 2nd century, B.C.E. under Shanakhdakheto guidance the nubians built the Temple F at Naqa, which has the unique feature of the first half of the temple; the interior partitions of the gods faced the back wall.

Warrior Queen Amanishakheto

10 BC to 1 A.D

After succeeding, Kandake (Queen) Amanirenas Amanishakheto was a strong, powerful woman and a great pyramid builder known to be extremely wealthy. The warrior queen of Nubia defeated a Roman Army sent by the first emperor of the Roman Empire, Augustus, who broke a peace treaty in his attempt to conquer Nubia. Her tomb at Meroë was one of the largest ever built. She is often portrayed on pyramid murals as a massive, powerful woman, covered with jewels, elaborate fringes, tasseled robes and carrying weapons in hand, preparing to lead her army.

Warrior Queen Amanirenas

Amanirenas qore li kdwe li

40 – 10 B.C.E

Queen Amanirenas was the ruler of the Kingdom of Kush (modern-day Sudan), Amanirenas, also known as Amanirena, who was one of the greatest kandakes who ruled over the Meroitic Kingdom of Kush in northeast Africa. Amanirenas was a brave warrior queen remembered for her loyal combat, side-by-side, with her soldiers. She and the Kushite army, along with her son Akinidad, took advantage and launched the initial attack on Egypt while Aelius Gallus, the Roman prefect of Egypt at the time of Roman rule, was away. She led her armies against the Romans in a war that lasted five years, from 27 BC to 22 B.C., successfully defeating the Roman forces in both Syene and Philae, although blinded in one eye. After a battle with Emperor Augustus, as an insult to him, she buried his statue under the entranceway of her palace so everyone could walk over it.

Queen Hatshepsut
"The Pharaoh"

Reigned from about 1473 to 1458 BCE

Queen Hatshepsut was born about 1503 BCE. She was part of the Eighteenth Dynasty, New Kingdom, a pharaoh ruler of Egypt, one of the very few women to hold that title. A temple was built in her honor at Deir el-Bahri (Dayru l-Bahri) near Thebes. We know Hatshepsut was well known during her lifetime for reinforcing how powerful she was.

Queen Tiye

"The Elder Lady"

20th dynasty

Queen Tiye "The Elder Lady" was very powerful during her husband's reign. In the 20th dynasty, she was the daughter of Yuya and Tjuyu. She was the Royal Wife of the Egyptian pharaoh Amenhotep III, the mother of Akhenaten and the grandmother of Tutankhamun (King Tut). Her husband devoted several shrines to her and constructed a temple for her in Sedeinga, Nubia, where she worshipped as a form of the goddess Hathor–Tefnut.

Queen Nzinga

Nzinga Mbande

1583 – 1663

Queen Nzinga (Nzinga Mbande) of the Ambundu Kingdoms of Ndongo and Matamba, located in present-day northern Angola, was born into the ruling family of Ndongo. Nzinga received military and political training as a child. The Mbundu people were resilient, and fought against the Portuguese and their expanding slave trade in Central Africa.

In the first meeting, Nzinga sought to establish her equality with the representative of the Portuguese. Noticing the only chair in the room belonged to Governor Corria, she immediately motioned to one of her assistants who fell on her hands and knees and served as a chair for Queen Nzinga for the rest of the meeting. Despite that display, Nzinga made accommodations with the Portuguese. She converted to Christianity and adopted the name, Dona Anna de Souza.

Empress Zewditu

1916-1930

Empress Zewditu of Ethiopia, Reign 1916-1930, was born on April 29, 1876, as Askala Maryam in the city of Harar in Enjersa Goro Province, Ethiopia. She was the first female head of an internationally recognized state in Africa in the 19th and 20th centuries, and the first Empress regnant of the Ethiopian Empire perhaps since the legendary Queen of Sheba (Makeba). Her reign was noted for the reforms of her Regent and designated heir Ras Tafari Makonnen (who succeeded her as Emperor Haile Selassie I). She was a conservative and held a strong religious devotion. Zewditu I was the daughter of Menelik II and would be the last monarch of direct agnatic descent from the Solomonic dynasty. She was a compassionate and kind woman, who became Empress because her nephew, Iyasu, had been excommunicated for apostasy. Even though he had treated her horribly, she still loved him and wept for him after being told she would take the throne over him.

Zewditu did promote the Ethiopian Orthodox Church and built temples throughout the Empire. She also allowed Mekonnen to abolish slavery and lead the Empire into the League of Nations.

Empress Taytu Betul

Empress of Ethiopia

1851 · 1918

E mpress of Ethiopia (1889–1913). She was the wife of Emperor Menelik II And was also the inspiration behind the 1896

Ethiopian victory against colonialism, in the battle of Adwa. Empress Taytu had a comprehensive education and was fluent in Ge'ez, the classical Ethiopian language. Empress Taytu is acknowledged to have carried considerable political power as the wife of Menelik, and the Emperor always consulted her before making important decisions. She fought in wars with men and women, and she is responsible for changing the name of Ethiopia's capital city from Finfinne to Addis Ababa.

Saint Escrava Anastacia

1740-?

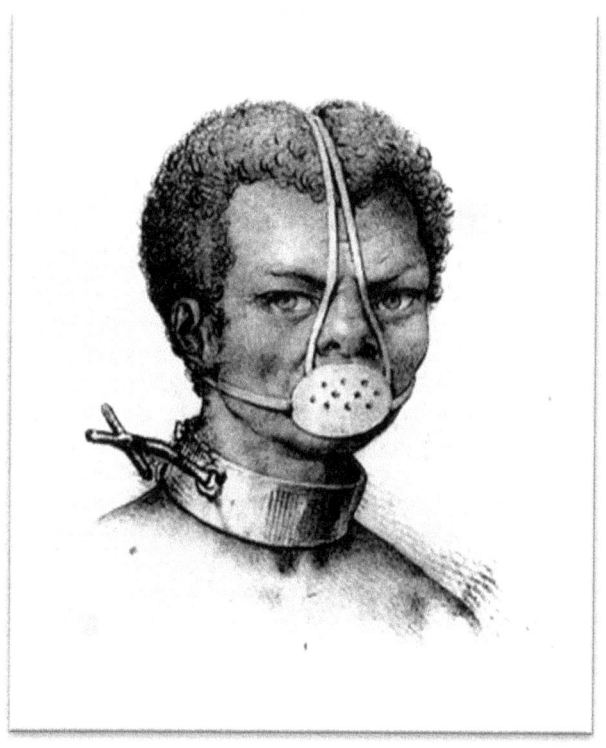

S aint Escrava Anastacia, born around 1740, an African Brazilian slave and martyred saint of Rio de Janeiro. She was the product of slave master rape and was born with piercing blue eyes. The slave master's wife oppressed Anastacia; because of her beauty and the miracles, she was made to wear an iron slave mask. Because of her Forgiving in spirit, Anastacia cured healed her master's son of mysterious illness before dying herself from tetanus caused by the very mask she was forced to wear. Saint Escrava Anastacia is a protector saint of the descendants of slaves and the poor in brazil.

Sargent Suzanne Belair
"The tigress of Haiti"
& Charles Belair,

The Haitian revolution,
August 22, 1791-1804

Suzanne Belair, known as Sanite Belair, was one of the female soldiers who fought during the Haitian Revolution. History fails to keep much about her early life. Sanite Belaire is now known as "L'Artibonite," Sanite, and her husband Charles Belair, is responsible for the uprising of almost the entire slave population of L'Artibonite, against their masters; the fierce Haitian woman who taught the African warriors of Haiti how to die with dignity after being captured and sentenced to death. Alongside her husband, the executioners tried to blindfold her because she was a woman. Sanite refused. She considered it an insult to be executed any differently than her husband. She watched as her husband was killed. Sanit Belè boldly presented her breast to receive the firing squad's fatal shots. It is said she shouted to the people "Viv Libète Anba esklavaj!"("Liberty, no to slavery!").

Nugaymath Turquia

1086 AD

D uring the Almoravid siege of Valencia after the death of the Cid, was a warrior queen called Nugaymath Turquia, the leader of three hundred Moorish African warriors. They were called the negresses and were members of the Almoravid Dynasties that occupied Spain in 1086 AD As described, their heads shaven, leaving hair only on the top and on a pilgrimage armed with Turkish bows." According to witnesses, King Bucar ordered that black African Moorish female warriors camp nearest to the town with all her Nugaymath soldiers; the Moorish women were so shrewd and master archers with the Turkish bow that it was a wonder to behold, and for that reason (the History) says that the Moors called her in Arabic nugaymath turquia, which means 'star of the archers of Turkey".

Cécile Fatiman

The Haitian revolution

August 22, 1791 to 1804

1771 - 1883

Cécile Fatiman was a warrior that led the slaves of Saint Domingue to fight for their freedom. Fatiman was married to Louis Michel Pierrot, a general in the Haitian revolutionary army and later president. She was a mambo, a high priestess in voodoo whose primary responsibility was maintaining the rituals and relationship between the spirits and the community. Cécile presided over a ceremony with hougon Dutty Boukman at the Bois Caïman in August 1791. During the ceremony, Cécile cut the throat of a pig, offered its blood to the attendees, who then drank it. They appeared to be possessed by the goddess Erzulie. Along with Dutty Boukman, Cécile urged the spectators to take vengeance against their French oppressors and "cast aside the image of the God of the oppressors." After, the ceremony at Bois Caïman Northern Saint-Domingue was in devastation as slaves pillaged, burned and killed across the region. On January 1, 1804, Saint-

Domingue became the independent Republic of Haiti, the first Black-led republic in the world.

Marie Saint Dédé Bazile

The Haitian Revolution

August 22,1791 to 1804

She was a woman who freed herself and did things even some men may have been hesitant to carry out. She had a close relationship with General Janjak Dessalines to supply frontline troops with food, ammunition and special ops movements. She took up arms in the Haitian Revolution at Bwa Kayiman and fought against the European slavers in Haiti. She also gathered the remains of Jean-Jacques Dessalines and gave him a proper burial after he was beaten and mutilated by his former comrades and left in the Pont Rouge bridge as garbage. She honored the father of a Black Nation and left us a legacy of courage.

Victoria Montou

The Haitian revolution
August 22, 1791-1804

Adbaraya Toya, known as Victoria Montou is originally from the Kingdom of Dahomey, currently Benin. She was a midwife, a warrior and a healer. She trained others in the art of war, including Haiti's founding father, Jean

Jacques Dessalines. Victoria Montou (known as "Aunt Toya") was a Dahomey warrior, also called N'Nonmiton, who was captured and brought to Haiti's sugar plantations. She used her skills to teach one of the greatest warriors that ever lived how to fight in hand-to-hand combat and how to throw a knife. Gran Toya guided Dessalines in his youth, and he called her "aunt." She was an extraordinary warrior, and as what would be considered an older woman, commanded her indigenous Haitian army after her freedom. In her last battle, she fought off three soldiers and was wounded severely. Before her death, she was able to see Haiti's victory, and she was revered for her bravery and laid to rest as Haiti's mother of independence.

Marie-Jeanneet Lamartiniére

The Haitian Revolution
August

22,1791 to 1804

RÉPUBLIQUE D'HAITI

MARIE-JEANNE ET LAMARTINIÈRE A LA CRÊTE A PIERROT

S
he served at the Battle of Crête-à-Pierrot alongside her husband in 1802 in the Haitian revolution. She fought in male uniform bearing both a rifle and a sword and was said to use the long rifle to snipe on the wounded French soldiers below with a skill all the men admired. Furthermore, she made a great impression with her fearlessness and courage. Lamartiniére boosted the morale of her colleagues with her bravery.

Princess Yennenga

The Svelte | 12th-century

P rincess Yennenga the Svelte was a famous horse-riding warrior who lived over 900 years ago. She was the daughter of Nedega, an early 12th-century king of the Dagomba Kingdom in what is now northern Ghana and whose son, Ouedraogo, founded the Mossi Kingdoms. Yennenga, the only daughter of Na Gbewa was a gorgeous princess. At the age of 14, she fought in the battle against the neighboring Malinkés. She was commander of her battalion and very brave, while skilled with javelins, spears and bows; in addition, she was an excellent horsewoman. When she reached an eligible age, her father refused her to marry. To express her unhappiness with her father, Yennenga planted a field of wheat, but when the crop grew, she let it rot. She would not harvest it. Her father was shocked and asked her for an explanation. "You see, father," she said, "you are letting me rot like the wheat in this field." Nedega failed to be moved by this gesture and locked her away. Yennenga is considered by the Mossi to be the mother of their empire, and many statues of her can be found in the capital city of Burkina Faso, Ouagadougou.

Breffu

1700's-1734

B reffu was from Ghana and enslaved in the danish West Indies. She worked on a sugar plantation in Coral Bay. After the danish defeated the local native Tainos, they began a slave trade, bringing primarily Africans from what is now Ghana. The sugar plantations were deathly, and many revolts began, many led by Breffu. One happened in 1733; hearing the signal of a cannon fired from Fort Frederiksen, Breffu entered the main house and killed both the plantation owner and his wife. Taking all gunpowder and ammunition, Breffu and her followers then proceeded to kill other members of the plantation owner's family. Under the leadership of Breffu, the plan of taking over the plantations was successful until the early part of 1734, when the French collaborated with the Danes to take back the island. She eventually committed suicide to evade capture. Her body was found at Browns Bay, along with another 23 rebels. After they examined the remains of the dead, they were surprised that

ELOGEIA HADLEY

Breffu was a woman. One plantation owner said:

"One of the leaders of the rebellion, Breffu, whom no one knew, we assumed to be a man having murdered my son and wife, is a WOMAN!"

Queen Dahia Al-Kahina

680's

D ahia Al-kahuna was a Berber Queen, then known as Numidia, in modern-day Algeria. She became the war leader of the Berber tribes in the 680s. She faced off with the

Islamic armies in their conquest of North Africa, at the end of the seventh century Dahia was active in the North African resistance to the Arab invasions of Africa. Around the year 690, she took personal command of the African armies. Under her leadership, the Arab legions retreated, regrouped and reassessed their strategy and tactics for the invasion of North Africa. Based on folklore, Dahia al-Kahina eventually took her own life rather than accept defeat at the hands of the Arabs. Her sons went on to help lead the Moorish invasion of Spain, but the death of this African woman ended what was perhaps the most determined and inspiring chapter in the effort to preserve Africa for the Africans.

Princess Amina of Zazzau

1533-1610

Princess Amina of Zazzau (present-day city of Zaria in Kaduna State). She ruled in the mid-sixteenth century in what is now the northwest region of Nigeria. The warrior Princess is a legend among the Hausa people for her military exploits. She controlled the trade routes in the region, erecting a network of commerce within the walls that surrounded Hausa cities within her dominion. According to the Kano Chronicle, she conquered as far as Nupe and Kwarafa, ruling for 34 years. Legend has it, Amina refused to marry and never bore children. Instead, it is said she took a temporary husband from the armies of conquered foes after every battle. After spending one night together, she would condemn him to death in the morning to prevent him from ever speaking about his sexual encounter with the Queen.

The Queen of Sheba, Makeda

Tenth Century B.C.E.

Archaeological evidence indicates that The Queen of Sheba, Makeda Sheba - is said to have lived as early as the tenth century B.C.E.. Sheba was a powerful incense-trading kingdom that prospered through trade with Jerusalem and the Roman empire. Makeda is immortalized in the Qur'an and the Bible, which describes her visit to Solomon "with a very great retinue, with camels bearing spices and very much gold and precious stones. Then she gave the king 120 talents of gold and a very great quantity of spices."

Queen Nandi

1760 - 1827

Queen Nandi was the daughter of Bhebhe, a former chief of the Langeni nation. Nandi was a mother of Shaka Zulu that went against social pressures. She was Queen mother of one of the Zulu kingdom's greatest kings. During the reign of her son, she had significant influence over the affairs of the Zulu nation. and became one of the most prevalent queens to date.

Queen Moremi Ajasoro
"The Spy Queen"
12ᵗʰ century

Moremi Ajasoro was the courageous Queen from the Lukugba compound in the Ile-Ife while her mother was a Princess from Offa. Moremi of Ile Ife saved her people from the Igbo forest raiders who would regularly disturb the city. Under the advice of the goddess of Esimirin, she should allow herself to be captured and go behind enemy lines and learn their secrets. While behind enemy lines, the ruler admired her beauty, so she was able to learn their ways. After escaping, she was able to give vital information to her people, and it helped end the raiders and defeat her enemies. As to celebrate the defeat, she went to thank the goddess, and instead of celebrating, the goddess wanted Moremi's only child as a sacrifice. Moremi's sacrifice helped with the preservation of the Yoruba nation.

The Dahomey Amazons or N'Nonmiton

1645 to 1904

ELOGEIA HADLEY

The Dahomey Amazons or N'Nonmiton were Fon female regiments of the army of the kingdom of Dahomey, beginning with King Houegbadja (who ruled from 1645 to 1685), the third King of Dahomey. From daughters to soldiers, from wives to weapons, they remain the only documented frontline all-female troops in modern warfare history. They were a band of African female warriors who left their European colonizers terrified; foreigners named them the Dahomey Amazons while they called themselves N'Nonmiton, which means "Our Mothers." Protecting their king on the bloodiest of battlefields, they emerged as an elite fighting force in the Kingdom of Dahomey, in the present-day Republic of Benin. Described as untouchable, sworn in as virgins, swift decapitation was their trademark.

Queen Mother Nana Yaa Asantewaa

of the Ejisu Clan of the Asante

1840 – 1921

During the Ashanti-British "War of the Golden Stool" and return of their king, Prempeh I had been exiled. The British demanded the Asante give them the golden stoole that held a great significance to the Asante people—disappointed with the council's response to resolve with the British. Queen Mother Nana Yaa Asantewaa made it clear that war was the only way, so she led an army of 5,000 women and men. While Yaa Asantewaa was captured by the British and deported, her bravery stirred a kingdom-wide movement for the return of Prempeh I and independence.

Her Speech-

"Now I see that some of you fear to go forward to fight for our king in the brave days of Osei Tutu, Okomfo Anokye and Opoku Ware, chiefs would not sit down to see their king be taken away without firing a shot. No European could have dared speak to leaders of Asante in the way the governor spoke to you this morning. Is it true that the bravery of Asante is no more? I cannot believe it. It cannot be! I must say this: if you, the men of Asante, will not go

forward, then we will. We, the women, will. I shall call upon my fellow women. We will fight! We will fight till the last of us falls in the battlefields."

Araminta Harriet Ross

"Harriet Tubman"

1822 – 1913

Was an African American abolitionist, humanitarian and Union spy during the

American Civil War. Born into slavery, Tubman escaped to Philadelphia in 1849, then immediately returned to Maryland to rescue her family. She made more than 19 missions to save more than 300 slaves with the help of the Underground Railroad. She later helped recruit men for John Brown's raid on Harpers Ferry on October 16-18, 1859, to free enslaved Blacks. In June 1863, Tubman became the first woman to lead an armed expedition in the Civil War. She guided the Combahee River Raid, which liberated more enslaved Blacks in South Carolina: the most massive liberation of enslaved Black people in American history.

Queen Nanny

18th century, 1686 – 1755

A Jamaican hero and leader of the Jamaican Maroons in the 18th century. Nanny was captured from Ghana, West Africa. She was intelligent and well respected as a spiritual leader woman who was instrumental in organizing the plans to free enslaved Africans. She and many others led several revolts across Jamaica for over 30 years; she freed more than 800 slaves and helped them settle into Maroon communities. She defeated the British in many battles, and despite repeated attacks from the British soldiers, Grandy Nanny's settlement, called Nanny Town, remained under Maroon control for several years.

Carlota Lukumi

1843-1844

Carlota was kidnapped from her Yoruba tribe, brought in chains to Cuba as a child and forced into slavery in the city of Matanzas, working to harvest sugar cane under the most brutal of conditions. She was bright, musical, determined and smart. In 1843, she and another enslaved woman named Fermina led an organized rebellion at the Triumvarato sugar plantation. Fermina was caught and locked up after her plans for the uprising were discovered. Using talking drums to communicate secretly, Carlota and her fellow warriors freed Fermina and dozens of others. They went on to wage a well-organized armed uprising against at least five brutal slave plantations.

Queen Gudit (Judith)

10th century 970 AD

Yodit, also called Judith, was a non-Christian, Ethiopian Queen of the 10th century 970AD. She resisted Christian conversion by Axumite evangelists. She was known for her destruction of the Axumite Empire. As the story goes, Yodit destroyed all in her path in Axum and its countryside, including churches and monuments. Yodit attempted to exterminate the members of the ruling Axumite dynasty and ended the dominance from over 700 years.

After Yodit successfully destroyed the Kingdom of Axum, she reigned over Ethiopia for four decades. In the seventh year of the reign of the Axumite Del-Nä'ad, she established a new dynasty that continued for three centuries. She expanded the border of Ethiopia West and South, including the provinces of Gojjam Begemder and up unto the Sidama provinces, where she was known as Ga'Ewa.

Queen Calafia

1510

S he was considered Queen of Diamonds and Gold, Califia and the California Blacks, a Queen that California named after of the black Mojave nations who lived in California before the Spanish invasion. Some say she was fictional, but many scholars believe that she was the ever-living Muurish Empress Calafia/Califia. Califia was the title of each empress. California was her land and she was known to be black of skin, of the muurish nationality, and ruled over Islands and Islands of black people, from California, Baja, to Hawaii. The first mention of this Queen was by western European Christians in the seventh century. It retold "The Song of Roland," where a passing mention of a place called California, the modern state of California, continues the legacy and the memory of this magnificent black Queendom and its Queen.

La Mulâtresse Solitude

1772 – 1802

L a Mulâtresse Solitude had joined the maroon settlement of La Goyave in the mid-1790s. During an attack by French General Desfouneaux, she became the leader of a small group that escaped to the hills of Guadeloupe, eluding capture When Napoleon Bonaparte enacted the law of May 20, 1802, reinstating slavery in the French colony Saint-Domingue, Guadeloupe, she was among those who rallied around Louis Delgrès and fought by his side for freedom. She survived the battle of May 28, 1802, but was caught and imprisoned by the French, because she was pregnant at the time of her imprisonment, her hanging was delayed until November 29 of the same year, one day after giving birth.

Tarenorerer

1800-1831

S he was born in Emu Bay, Van Diemen's Land, as a member of the Tommeginne people. she was a kidnapper and sold. During her captivity, she learned to speak English and how to use firearms. Her brothers and two of her sisters joined her with the sealers. Later, she was able to return to Tasmania, where she gathered a guerrilla band of indigenous warriors of both sexes and lead them against the colonists. As she was able to train them in using firearms, they were successful. They were referred to as an Amazon. Tarenorerer escaped to Port Sorell with her brothers and two sisters but was captured by sealers and taken to the Hunter Islands. They were then taken to Bird Island to catch seals and mutton birds. Eventually, she was arrested and imprisoned, and she died of influenza in prison.

Nehanda Charwe Nyakasikana

Spiritualist

1840-1898

Nehanda Charwe Nyakasikana was a spiritualist leader known as a spirit medium and mhondoro ("lion spirit"). At birth, Nehanda Nyakasikana was to be the female incarnation of the great oracle Nehanda. Based on the beliefs of the Shona people, the spirits of the great-great ancestors, are still among them as supernatural protectors. Such great spirits were called mhondoro or lions' spirits. These spirits were amongst the most powerful, as they were responsible for giving advice to several tribes, ensuring peace, as well as presiding over ceremonies and rituals.

European settlers began to travel to the region from Britain during Nehanda Nyakasikana's rule, imposing a "hut tax" and forced labor camps for both the Ndebele and Shona people. These rules and laws caused the Matabele Rebellion. This war lasted against colonial settlers 1896-1897 and after the battle, Nehanda was captured and charged with murder and sentenced to death. Nehanda's heroism became a significant source of inspiration in the nation's struggle for liberation in the 1960s and 1970s. Nehanda is referred to as Mbuya Nehanda and described as the grand-mother of present-day Zimbabwe. Her last words will never be forgotten, "Mapfupa angu achamuka! (my bones will surely rise!)".

Sojourner Truth

1797-1883

S ojourner Truth, born Isabella Baumfree November 26, 1797, was a women's rights activist. Truth was born in Swartekill, Ulster County, New York, but escaped with her infant daughter in 1826. After going to court to recover her son in 1828, she became the first black woman to win such a case against a white man. Isabella changed her name to Sojourner in 1843 after she became convinced that God had called her to leave the city and go into the countryside, "testifying the hope that was in her regarding her best-known controversial poem- delivered in 1851, at the Ohio Women's Rights Convention in Akron, Ohio. The address became widely known during the Civil War.

MARY FIELDS

"Stagecoach Mary"

1832 - 1914

M ary Fields, or "Stagecoach Mary," was the first African American woman who worked as a mail carrier in the United

States; and the second African American woman to work for the United States Postal Service. The six-foot, 200-pound woman was known to carry a jug of whiskey and a pistol under her work apron. In 1894, Stagecoach Mary and her mother opened a restaurant in Cascade, Montana. Mary Fields' legacy is still represented in the city of Cascade.

Queen Liliuokalani Honolulu, Last Black Queen

September 2, 1838 - November 11, 1917

Honolulu LAST BLACK QUEEN Liliuokalani, original name Lydia Kamakaeha, also called Lydia Liliuokalani Paki or Liliu Kamakaeha, was the first and only reigning Hawaiian queen and the last Hawaiian sovereign to govern the islands, which were occupied by Americans in 1898. She served as regent during King Kalakaua's world tour in 1881. During a world tour in 1887, she was received by U.S. Pres. Grover Cleveland and by Britain's Queen Victoria. On the death of King Kalakaua in January 1891, Liliuokalani ascended the throne, becoming the first woman ever to occupy it. The last native ruler of Hawaii was celebrated following the queen's ascension to the throne on January 29, 1891. She was described as "strong and resolute." She had earlier made her position clear by opposing the renewed Reciprocity Treaty of 1887, signed by Kalakaua, granting privileged commercial concessions to the United States and ceding to them the port of Pearl Harbor. This attitude forever alienated her from Hawaii's haole foreign businessmen who, after her accession, tried to abrogate her authority. Dole, however, defied the order, claiming that Cleveland did not have the authority to interfere. In 1895 an insurrection in the queen's name, led by royalist Robert Wilcox, was suppressed by Dole's group, and Liliuokalani was kept under house arrest on charges of treason. On January 24, 1895, to win pardons for her supporters who had been jailed following the revolt, she agreed to sign a formal abdication. As head of the 'Onipa' or resolute movement, whose motto was "Hawaii for the Hawaiians," Liliuokalani fought bitterly against the takeover of the islands by the United States. Annexation, nonetheless, occurred in July 1898. In that year, she published Hawaii's Story by Hawaii's Queen and composed "Aloha Oe," a song ever afterward beloved in the islands. Thereafter, she withdrew from public life, enjoying a government pension and the homage of islanders and visitors alike.

Ida Bell Wells

Journalist and Abolitionist

1862 - 1931

In the 1890s, Ida B Wells, a journalist, and abolitionist led an anti-lynching crusade in the

United States. She went on to find and become integral in groups striving for African American justice. Wells wrote articles decrying the lynching of her friend and the wrongful deaths of other African Americans. Putting her own life at risk, she spent two months traveling in the South, gathering information on other lynching incidents.

Aline Sitoe Diatta

"The Joan of Arc of Africa"

1920 – 1944

Aline Sitoé Diatta was born sometime around 1920, in the village of Kabrousse in Casamance in Senegal. She was orphaned young and lived with her uncle until his death, after which she moved to the village to work. Her people were the Djola. The Portuguese founded a trade of wax, ivory, skins and slavery. In the 17th century, they created a port that later developed the region's capital, Ziguinchor and after the Portuguese in 1942, the French began seizing rice fields and other property. When Aline was 21, she heard a voice telling her to return to her village at once to free her people from the colonialists. The voice added that if she failed to do so, bad luck would befall her. Aline ignored the voice. Four days later, she woke up paralyzed, possibly from a stroke, quite rare for someone so young. Aline finally requested to be turned back to Casamance. No sooner was she returned to the village than the paralysis left her. She would retain a limp from her ordeal.

Aline began to take the voices seriously. Soon, she was encouraging her people to return to their Djola roots and caste system, no griots (storytellers/historical class), no slaves, no nobility class; theirs was a rare egalitarian society. They were highly respectful too, integrated with nature and adept at herbal medicine. Moreover, they were of a musical culture, as their instruments played a significant part in their many rituals. These rituals favored a strong sense of collectivism.

The Djola also resisted either Christian or Islamic conversion, Aline's indignation at the injustices were perpetrated by them. She encouraged her people to disobey French orders, to avoid paying taxes to the French and to avoid joining the French army. At first, her people did not believe her. She was told to prove that her voices were divine. "Why not make it rain?" they asked. At this, Aline suggested incantations along with animal sacrifices. Following these ceremonies, water descended upon the rice fields. Aline was proclaimed a true divine servant. The message spread beyond the region, and it was told that she healed and that by merely touching her, the sick was restored to health. Many, all over Senegal, made pilgrimages to meet her, the return to tradition and roots. Aline's name reached the French, a woman that could rally the Senegalese against them. She had to be eliminated for inciting rebellion and for refusing to submit to the established order. Aline was ultimately captured by the French and later died while held captive.

ELOGEIA HADLEY

INFLUENCERS & SHEROES

2

Black Women all over the world were examples of strength and power, even in the face of adversity. Many have set a standard of excellence, yet they stay humble and grounded in their brilliance. And here are a few women that continue to be the sheroes, queens, and warriors from the past and present.

Fannie Lou Hamer,

Political Activist, Sharecropper and Organizer

Fannie Lou Hamer made a decision that changed her life and the lives of others. In the summer of 1962, she decided to attend a local meeting held by the Student Non-Violent Coordinating Committee (SNCC), who encouraged African Americans to register to vote. On August 31, 1962, she traveled with 17 others to the county courthouse in Indianola to achieve this goal. They encountered harassment by law enforcement. However, they continued, and only Hamer and one other person were allowed to fill out an application. Because this attempt to vote came at a high price for Hamer, she was fired from her job and forced from the plantation she had called home—just for registering to vote. She went on to become a speaker of the fair treatment of blacks in America.

Winnie Mandela
Apartheid Activist and Politician

September 1936 – 2 April 2018

Born as Kosikazi Nobandle Nomzamo Madikizela, South Africa's first black professional social welfare worker, who chose service to needy people and devotion of her energy and skill to the struggle for equality and justice for all people in South Africa. After her marriage to Nelson Mandela in 1958, she suffered harassment, imprisonment, and periodic banishment for her continuing involvement in that struggle.

Folorunsho Alakija

Entrepreneur and Businesswoman

Folorunsho Alakija stepped into the business arena in the late 70's. She makes her wealth through her fashion label and her oil company. To make fashion her top priority, Folorunsho Alakija quit her role as a secretary at a Nigerian bank. She then relocated to Europe, where she studied fashion on a full-time basis. After completing her fashion course in Europe, Folorunsho Alakija returned to Nigeria and set up Supreme Stitches –a fashion label that provides Nigerian female dignitaries with fashion needs. With her wealth still soaring high, Folorunsho Alakija is presently worth $1.6 billion.

Ava Marie DuVernay

Filmmaker

She is an American filmmaker and the first black woman to win several awards for directing. She has won the dramatic competition at the 2012 Sundance Film Festival for her second feature film, *Middle of Nowhere*. She also won for her work on Selma. DuVernay is also the first black woman to be nominated for a Golden Globe Award for Best Director, the first black female director to have her film nominated for the Academy Award for Best Picture. In 2017, she was nominated for the Academy Award for Best Documentary Feature for her film *13th*.

Shirley A Chisholm

Congresswoman

Shirley Chisholm was the first African American congresswoman in 1968. She was also the first woman and African American to seek the nomination for president of the United States from one of the two major political parties in 1972. Her motto and title of her auto-biography—Unbossed and Unbought—illustrated her outspoken advocacy for women and minorities during her seven terms in the U.S. House of Representatives.

Claudette Colvin
Civil Rights Activist

Before Rosa Park, many fought against segregation, and Colvin was one who refused to give up her bus seat to a white passenger. Colvin was riding home on a city bus after school when a bus driver told her to give up her seat to a white passenger. She refused, saying, "It's my constitutional right to sit here as much as that lady. I paid my fare, it's my constitutional right." Colvin stood her ground. "I felt like Sojourner Truth was pushing down on one shoulder and Harriet Tubman was pushing down on the other—saying, 'Sit down girl!' I was glued to my seat." Colvin was arrested on several charges, including violating the city's segregation laws. She sat in jail, terrified. "I was really afraid because you just didn't know what white people might do at that time," Colvin later said. Colvin was bailed out by her minister and her family did not sleep because of possible retaliation. The NAACP-The National Association for the Advancement of Colored took Colvin's case to challenge the segregation laws, but they decided against it because she was a young single mother. Colvin became one of four plaintiffs in the Browder v. Gayle case. The decision in the 1956 case, which had been filed by Fred Gray and Charles D. Langford on behalf of the African American women, ruled that Montgomery's segregated bus system was unconstitutional. Two years later, Colvin moved to New York City, where she had her second son, Randy, and worked as a nurse's aide at a Manhattan nursing home. She retired in 2004.

Maya Angelou
Author Actress and Poet

Maya Angelou was an American author, actress, screenwriter and civil rights activist known for her nonfiction biography; *I Know Why the Caged Bird Sings*. She made literary history as the first bestseller by an African American woman. Angelou was also a dancer and poet who received several honors, including two NAACP Image Awards in the exceptional literary work, nonfiction category, in 2005 and 2009.

Toni Morrison
College Professor and Author

Toni Morrison, born Chloe Anthony Wofford, was an African American novelist, essayist, book editor and college professor. Her first novel, *The Bluest Eye*, was published in 1970 and known for her examination of black experiences, specifically, the black female's life within the community and the world. She received the Nobel Prize for Literature in 1993.

Zora Neale Hurston
Writer and Anthropologist

Zora Neale Hurston was a writer and anthropologist, a fixture of the Harlem Renaissance and author of 'Their Eyes Were Watching God and *Mules of Men'*. Zora Neale Hurston was popular during New York City's Harlem Renaissance, due to her novels like *Their Eyes Were Watching God* and shorter works like "*Sweat.*" She was an outstanding folklorist and anthropologist who recorded cultural history and black life. Hurston died in poverty in 1960, before a revival of interest led to posthumous recognition of her accomplishments, but in recent years, other authors had many of her work published.

Yolande Cornelia "Nikki" Giovanni
Poet and Educator

She is an American poet, writer, commentator, activist and educator. One of the world's most well-known African American poets; her work includes poetry anthologies, poetry recordings and nonfiction essays, covering topics ranging from race and social issues to children's literature. She has won numerous awards, including the Langston Hughes Medal and the NAACP Image Award. She has been nominated for a Grammy Award for her poetry album, The Nikki Giovanni Poetry Collection.

Angela Davis
Writer, Activist and Educator

Writer, activist and educator Angela Davis was born on January 26, 1944, in Birmingham, Alabama. She grew up in a middle-class neighborhood dubbed "Dynamite Hill" due to many of the African American homes in the area that were bombed by the Ku Klux Klan. Davis is best known as a radical African American educator and activist for civil rights and other social issues. She knew about racial prejudice from her experiences with discrimination growing up in Alabama. As a teenager, Davis organized study groups, which were broken up by the authorities.

Assata Shakur

Activist

She is an African American activist who was a member of the Black Panther Party (BPP) and Black Liberation Army (BLA) between 1971 and 1973. Assata worked through the BPP and the BLA to fight racial, social and economic oppression. Shakur is a revolutionary Black icon, whose legend has evolved into making her a patron saint of Black rebellion in the last half-century. She was serving a sentence for allegedly killing a New Jersey state trooper in 1973 in self-defense. The Queens, N.Y, native has been living in Cuba for over 40 years after having escaped from the prison.

Dr. Francis Cress Welsing
Psychiatrist and Author

F rances Luella Cress was a psychiatrist and author. She was born in Chicago, then later moved to Washington, D.C. and worked at many hospitals, especially children's hospitals. While Welsing was an assistant professor at Howard University, she published her first body of work, "The Cress Theory of Color-Confrontation," in 1974. Two years later, she released The Isis Papers, a compilation of essays she has written about global and local race relations. Dr. Francis Cress Welsing lectured until she passed away in 2016.

Queen Afua

Wellness Coach, Holistic Healer, Author

Queen Afua, based in New York City, is a wellness coach, holistic healer, author and health practitioner for over 40 years. She is a pioneer of self-care and the green food movement, CEO of the Queen Afua Wellness Center and founder of the Heal Thyself product line. She is also a Shrine of Ptah initiate, a Nebt-Het Temple and Afrakan Order Chief Purification Priestess, as well as a Khamitic (Egyptian) Priestess. One of many of her most significant works written is *"Heal Thyself."*

Dr. Joy Degruy
Clinical Psychologist and Author

D r. Joy DeGruy is a Clinical Psychologists academic, researcher, who served as assistant professor at the Portland State University School of Social Work. She is current the president and CEO of DeGruy Publications, Inc. Dr. Degruy is also an acclaimed author of *"Post Traumatic Slave Syndrome* — America's Legacy of Enduring Injury and Healing"*, with a second book in the works, *"Post Traumatic Slave Syndrome Part 2: Be The Healing".* She is also one of the first and only clinical psychologists that began the research on cognitive dissonance during slavery which led her to the theory that explains the adaptive survival behaviors in African American and communities throughout and the Diaspora.

Maxine Waters

Congresswoman

Congresswoman Maxine Waters was Elected in November 2018 to her fifteenth term in the U.S. House of Representatives in the 43rd Congressional District of California and is considered by many to be one of the most powerful women in American politics today. She has gained a reputation as an outspoken advocate for women, children, people of color and the poor. Congresswoman Waters serves as a member of the Steering & Policy Committee and is the Co-Chair of the bipartisan Congressional Task Force on Alzheimer's Disease. She is also a member of the Congressional Progressive Caucus, and a member and past chair of the Congressional Black Caucus. Throughout her more than 40 years of public service, she has been tackling difficult and often controversial issues.

Dr. Patricia A. Newton

Psychiatrist, Scholar, Lecturer

She was an international psychiatrist, scholar, lecturer, published author, pioneer and traditional Ghanaian Royal. Dr. Patricia Newton stood strong as an African-centered psychiatrist who understood the importance of both psychiatry and psychology. She saw that the trauma Black people faced had both environmental and chemical origins. Dr. Newton founded the Black Psychiatrists of America in Maryland. Through that organization, her writings, appearances and community outreach, Dr. Newton redefined how we look a Black psychiatry today. In 1969, she founded the Black Psychiatrists of America (BPA) to create resources for psychiatrists who recognize that European psychiatry training is inadequate to address the healing of Black people. Dr. Patricia Newton passed away on September 27, 2020.

Carol Moseley Braun
Senator

Born Aug. 16, 1947, Democratic senator from Illinois (1993–99), the first African American woman elected to the U.S. Senate. After receiving her law degree, she married Michael Braun in 1973 and worked as an assistant U.S. attorney before her election to the Illinois House of Representatives in 1978. During her 10 years, she became known for her advocacy of health care, education reform, and gun control. She was named an assistant leader for the Democratic majority. From 1988 to 1992 Moseley Braun served as Cook County (Illinois) recorder of deeds. Displeased with U.S. Senator Alan Dixon's support of U.S. Supreme Court nominee Clarence Thomas, she ran against Dixon in the 1992 Democratic primary and won an upset victory over Dixon on her way to capturing a seat in the Senate. From 1999 to 2001 she served as U.S. ambassador to New Zealand. She unsuccessfully sought the Democratic Party presidential nomination in 2004 as well as run for mayor of Chicago. Moseley Braun founded (2005) an organic food company.

Michelle Alexander

Professor, Writer, Civil Rights Advocate

Michelle Alexender (born October 7, 1967) is a writer, civil rights advocate and visiting professor at Union Theological Seminary (New York City). She is best known for her 2010 book *The New Jim Crow: Mass Incarceration in the Age of Colorblindness* and is an opinion columnist for The New York Times. Alexander served as director of the Racial Justice Project at the ACLU of Northern California from 1998 to 2005, which led a national campaign against racial profiling by law enforcement. She directed the Civil Rights Clinic at Stanford Law School and was a law clerk for Justice Harry Blackmun at the U. S. Supreme Court and for Chief

Judge Abner Mikva on the United States Court of Appeals for the D.C. Circuit. As an associate at Saperstein, Goldstein, Demchak & Baller, she specialized in plaintiff-side class-action suits alleging race and gender discrimination. Alexander sits on the faculty of Union Theological Seminary in the City of New York, as a Visiting Professor of Social Justice. In 2018, she was hired as an opinion columnist for The New York Times.

Ama Ata Aidoo

Educator and Writer

Ama Ata Aidoo was born in a small village in Ghana's central Fanti-speaking region in 1942. She studied literature at the University of Ghana and became a university lecturer. There, she produced her first play in 1964. In January 1982, she was appointed Minister of Education. As Minister, Aidoo wanted to make education in Ghana freely accessible to all - but after 18 months when she realized that she couldn't achieve these goals, she resigned. She moved to Zimbabwe to become a full-time writer and also lived and taught in the USA. She has won many literary awards including the 1992 Commonwealth Writers Prize for Best Book (Africa) for Changes.

Zenzile Miriam Makeba

Singer, Goodwill Ambassador and Civil Rights Activist

March 4, 1932 to November 9, 2008

Also known as Mama Africa, Miriam Makeba was a singer from South Africa, as well as a songwriter, actress, United Nations' goodwill ambassador and civil rights activist. Associated with musical genres including Afro-pop, jazz, and world music, she was an advocate against apartheid in South Africa.

Tamika Danielle Mallory
Activist and Organizer

T amika, (born June 8, 1980) is an American activist and organizer of the 2017 Women's March, which she and her three other co-chairs She became a staff member of the National Action Network at the age of 15 and spent time working closely with the Obama Administration on gun control legislation. Mallory is a proponent of feminism, and the 'Black Lives Matter' movement. Tamika Mallory is Nationally recognized as a social justice champion. Her activism has gained her many followers. Tamika Mallory continues the fight for social justice.

Candace Owens
Political Activist and Commentator

C andace Owens is a bold, conservative political activist and commentator. She is best known for her pro-republican commentary and critical stance on the Democratic Party. She promotes black conservatism and launched an anti-cyberbullying website called SocialAutopsy.com. Owens has served the American conservative non-profit organization, Turning Point USA and was inducted into the organization as director of urban engagement and later served as its "Communications Director." She launched the Blexit movement to convince African Americans to leave the Democratic Party and register as Republicans. She hosts the Candace Owens Hour program on the American non-profit organization's PragerU's YouTube channel.

Alicia Garza, Patrisse Cullors and Opal Tometi

Political Activists and Organizers

In 2013, three black women organized and created a Black-centered political movement called Black Lives Matter. It was in response to the acquittal of Trayvon Martin's murderer. The project is now a global network of 40 plus chapters. Our members organize local power to intervene in violence inflicted on Black communities by the state and vigilantes. Black Lives Matter is an ideological and political intervention in a world where Black lives are systematically targeted. It is an affirmation of Black folks' humanity, our contributions to this society and our resilience in the face of deadly oppression.

Sistah Soulja
Author and "Raptivist"

Born Lisa Williamson

Known in the hip hop community as a self-proclaimed "raptivist" who released an album, "360 Degrees of Power," in 1992 via Epic Records. She is also an author, activist, recording artist and film producer, and one of the hip-hop's most influential female gurus. She prides herself on speaking up for the youth. A graduate of Rutgers University, she earned a degree in American History and African Studies. She also attended the Cornell University Advanced Placement Study Program and studied abroad in Europe at the University of Salamanca. Sister Souljah has traveled throughout the world over the years. Sistah Souljah continues to write and be a beacon of light in her community.

Ruby Bridges
Activist
September 8, 1954

Ruby Bridges, (born September 8, 1954, Tylertown, Mississippi, U.S.), American activist. Ruby Bridges was six when she became the first African American child to integrate into a white Southern elementary school. She later became a civil rights activist. On November 14, 1960, she was escorted to class by her mother and U.S. marshals due to violent mobs. Bridges' brave act was a milestone in the civil rights movement, and she continues to share her story in educational forums all over the United States.

Ella Baker

Community Organizer and Political Activist

December 13, 1903 –

December 13, 1986

E lla Josephine Baker was an American community organizer and political activist who brought her skills and principles to bear in the major civil rights organizations of the mid-20th century. In the early 1930s, in one of her first efforts at implementing social improvement, she helped organize the Young Negroes Cooperative League, which was created to form cooperative groups that would pool community resources and thus provide less-expensive goods and services to members. Baker married T.J. Roberts in the late 1930s and then joined the staff of the National Association for the Advancement of Colored People (NAACP), first as a field secretary and later as national director of the NAACP's various branches. Unhappy with the bureaucratic nature of the NAACP and newly responsible for the care of her young niece, she resigned from her director position in 1946, but worked with the New York branch to integrate local schools and improve the quality of education for black children. In 1955, Baker cofounded the organization In Friendship to raise money for the civil rights movement in the South. In 1957, she met with a group of Southern black ministers and helped form the Southern Christian Leadership Conference (SCLC) to coordinate reform efforts throughout the South. Martin Luther King, Jr., served as the SCLC's first president and Baker as its director. She left the SCLC in 1960 to help student leaders of college activist groups organize the Student Nonviolent Coordinating Committee (SNCC). With her guidance and encouragement,

SNCC became one of the foremost advocates for human rights in the country. Her influence was reflected in the nickname she acquired: "Fundi," a Swahili word meaning a person who teaches a craft to the next generation. Baker continued to be a respected and influential leader in the fight for human and civil rights until her death on her 83rd birthday.

Dorothy "Dot" Counts-Scoggins

Educator and Activist

March 25, 1942-Present

Dorothy Counts, born March 25, 1942, was one of the first black students integrated in Harry Harding High School in Charlotte, North Carolina, as part of the initial effort to desegregate schools in that city in response to the U.S. Supreme Court's ruling of racial segregation as unconstitutional in Brown v. Board of Education (1954). In 1956 forty black students applied to transfer to white schools across the state; she was the only black student assigned to Harry Harding High School. On the first day she was scheduled to attend, the harassment began. Much of it was orchestrated by leaders of the segregationist

White Citizens Council, which urged the boys attending the school to block her entry and the girls of the school to spit on her. Counts walked to the Harding High School through angry crowds who hurled insults, while some threw rocks and others spat on her. More abuse followed while teachers ignored the incident. Count's family also received threatening phone calls, then her parents withdrew her from the school over safety. The attempt at desegregation failed. Count's parents sent her to Philadelphia to continue her education and she later attended John C. Smith University from which she earned a degree in 1965. Counts then began her professional career in childcare services. In 2008, Harding High School awarded Counts an honorary diploma. In 2010, Counts received a public apology from one member of the crowd who had harassed her in 1957 and renamed its library in honor of Dorothy Counts.

Audley Moore
"Queen Mother"
Civil Rights Activist
Jul 27, 1898 - May 02, 1997

Moore was a prominent Harlem civil rights activist, born on July 27, 1898, in New Iberia, Louisiana to Ella and St. Cry Moore. She was self-educated and a follower of the Marcus Garvey movement, while living in Harlem New York 1922, during the Harlem renaissance. While in Harlem, she became a member and then a leader within Garvey's Universal Negro Improvement Association (UNIA). A proud shareholder in the Black Star Line, she helped organize UNIA conventions in New York. After the demise of the UNIA, Moore founded several organizations. With her base in Harlem, Moore founded and served as president of the Universal Association of Ethiopian Women in 1950. In 1963, she founded the Committee for Reparations for Descendants of U.S. Slaves, and The Republic of New Africa, which demanded self-determination, land and reparations for black people in America. During the height of the Cold War, Moore presented a petition to the United Nations in 1957, which demanded land and billions in reparations for people of African descent and it requested direct support for African Americans who sought to immigrate to Africa.

In 1966, she participated in a sit-in at a Board of Education meeting in Brooklyn 1966. She also served as the bishop of the Apostolic Orthodox Church of Judea and she co-founded the Commission to Eliminate Racism, Council of Churches of Greater New York. While attending the funeral of former Ghanaian President Kwame Nkrumah in 1972, the Ashanti Nation bestowed upon her the honorary title "Queen Mother." Queen Mother Moore's activism continued through the mid-1990s, and she made her final public appearance at the Million Man March in 1995. On May 2, 1997, Queen Mother Moore passed away at the age of 98 from natural causes in Brooklyn.

Josephine Baker
Activist, Spy, and Entertainer
June 03, 1906 - April 12, 1975

In 1925, Josephine Baker took Paris, France by storm, appearing on stage in "La Revue Negre" wearing nothing but a skirt of artificial bananas in Danse Sauvage. Born Josephine Freda MacDonald in St. Louis, Missouri on June 3, 1906, at 13, she packed up and left to perform on the road. She was considered too young and too skinny to be a chorus girl but did non-performing work. Her big break came on October 2, 1925, when she opened in "La Revue Negre" at the Theatre des Champs-Elysees. Baker exploited European colonial fantasies of the Africans, brought jazz and the Charleston to Paris and soon became known for her uninhibited performances and costumes. In 1931, Baker released J'ai Deux amours, which became her most successful recording and performing several films. Ernest Hemingway, F. Scott Fitzgerald, Pablo Picasso, Langston Hughes and Christian Dior all announced themselves fans of Baker after seeing her performances.

In 1936 Baker's success in Europe did not carry over to the United States; the American audiences did not embrace her performances. Josephine Baker also faced racial discrimination in the United States. In protest, Baker renounced her American citizenship and moved permanently to Paris in 1937. During World War II, Josephine Baker used her fame as an entertainer to gather intelligence for the French Resistance during the Nazi occupation. she carried sensitive documents to neutral countries and allied occupied areas, sometimes using invisible ink on sheet music. After the war, Baker was decorated for her work by the French government. She adopted orphans from around the world whom she called her "Rainbow Tribe." In August 1963, Baker was one of only two women to speak at the March on Washington. Josephine Baker died in Paris on April 12, 1975, and was buried in Monaco; she was the first American woman to receive French military honors at her funeral.

BILLIE HOLIDAY
Entertainer and Singer
April 07, 1915 - July 17, 1959

Born as Eleanora Fagan In 1930, Holiday began singing in local clubs and renamed herself "Billie" after the film star Billie Dove. At the age of 18, Holiday was discovered by producer John Hammond while she was performing in a Harlem jazz club, where she was known for her distinctive melancholy voice. Holiday went on to record with jazz pianist Tedd. She made several singles, including "What a Little Moonlight Can Do" and "Miss Brown to You." That same year, Holiday appeared with Duke Ellington in the film *Symphony* in Black. Holiday met and befriended saxophonist Lester Young, who was part of Count Basie's orchestra on and off for years.

He even lived with Holiday and her mother for a while. Young gave Holiday the nickname "Lady Day" in 1937 becoming one of the first female African American vocalists to work with a white orchestra. Promoters, however, objected to Holiday for being black and for her unique vocal style, so she left the orchestra out of frustration. Holiday performed at New York's Café Society and developed some of her trademark stage personas there, wearing gardenias in her hair and singing with her head tilted back. At this time, Holiday also debuted two of her most famous songs, "God Bless the Child" and "Strange Fruit." Her record company, Columbia was not interested in "Strange Fruit," which was a story of the lynching of black people in the South. "Strange Fruit" is considered to be one of her signature ballads, and due to the controversy, that surrounded it, some radio stations banned the record. It is said the government also warned her about singing that song in public. Holiday gave her final performance

ELOGEIA HADLEY

in New York City on May 25, 1959. Not long after this event, Billie Holiday died of pulmonary edema and heart failure caused by cirrhosis of the liver on July 17, 1959, liver failure.

Eartha Kitt
Entertainer and Activist

*January 17, 1927 –
December 25, 2008*

E artha Kitt, born Eartha Mae Keith on January 17, 1927 and died December 25, 2008,. She was an African American singer, actress, comedienne, dancer, and activist who became popular in Paris as a nightclub singer, then returned to the United States to appear in films and on Broadway. Her 1953 recording of "Santa Baby" is still a favorite today. In the 1960s, Kitt had a recurring role as Cat woman on TV's Batman, but her career waned after she criticized the Vietnam War during a luncheon with Lady Bird Johnson. Eartha Kitt had a difficult childhood. She found fame in the New York school of performing arts where she won awards and scholarships leading to travel. She was discovered in Europe by actor-director Orson Welles. Welles, who reportedly called her "the most exciting woman alive," cast her as Helen of Troy in his production of Dr. Faustus. The recording featured such signature songs as "I Want to Be Evil" and "C'est Si Bon," as well as the perennially holiday classic "Santa Baby." On the big screen, Kitt starred opposite Nat King Cole in the W. C. Handy biopic St. Louis Blues (1958). She netted her only Academy Award nomination the following year, for her role as the title character in Anna Lucasta. In the film, Kitt plays a sassy young woman who is forced to use her womanly wiles to survive, starring opposite Sammy Davis Jr. In the late 1960s, Kitt played one of her most famous parts — the villainous vixen "Cat woman." She took over the role, in the TV series Batman, from Julie Newmar. Remarkably, Kitt only played Cat woman on a handful of episodes of the short-lived show, then Kitt found herself in a media firestorm in 1968. She attended a luncheon about juvenile delinquency and crime hosted by Lady Bird Johnson at the White House. At the event, Kitt shared her thoughts on the matter, telling the First Lady that "You send the best of this country off to be shot and maimed," according to the Washington Post. "No wonder the kids rebel and take the pot." Her remarks against the Vietnam War offended Johnson and made headlines. However, in the 1980s she was invited back to the White House by President Jimmy Carter. She eventually continued her career throughout the 80s and 90s.

Esther Jones
Betty Boop
Dancer and Entertainer
1919-1934

Betty Boop is one of the most iconic cartoon characters of all time, a virtual sex symbol created during a time when bold women were often frowned upon. The character's signature vocals stood out, but she wouldn't exist if it weren't for a Black child star and performer from Harlem who inspired the style. Esther Jones was a singer in who performed regularly in the Cotton Club jazz establishment. Jones, also known as "Baby Esther," coined a vocal style using "boops" and another childlike scat sounds during her act. Actress Helen Kane caught a Baby Esther performance in the late 1920s and began using the "boops" in her songs as well. Kane found fame early on with songs such as "I Wanna Be Loved by You" and incorporated the "Boop A Doop" scat, often called the "baby-style," into her music. In 1930, cartoonist Max Fleischer introduced the Betty Boop character via Paramount Studios' Talkatoon series. Some historians point to Kane as the inspiration, a fact backed up during an episode of the television history talk series, Stu's Show.

BESSIE STRINGFIELD

"The Motorcycle Queen"

1911 - February 16, 1993

Betsy Ellis Springfield was born in 1911. Springfield rode her motorcycle around the Americas from 1929 until she died in 1993. She defied several stereotypes about what black women could do. Springfield rode across the country on a motorcycle 10 years after women gained the right to vote. The American interstate highway system wouldn't even be proposed until 1956, so her travels took her the slow way, on regional roads and highways through towns that were often not friendly to blacks. African Americans were not welcome in almost any motel across the country, so she often stayed with black families she met along the way or slept on her bike. Springfield was the first black woman to ride a motorcycle in every one of the lower 48 states and made motorcycle trips in other countries. including Europe. While her first bike was an Indian Scout model, Springfield soon discovered that she loved Harleys, which became her bike of choice; she owned 27 in her lifetime. Springfield became an asset to the United States government during World War II, as a motorcycle dispatcher, despite being a civilian woman. In her lifetime, she won numerous awards and worked as a nurse. She even wowed the crowds on her way to church riding on her motorcycle.

Oprah Winfrey

Talk Show Host, and Television Producer

Her primary source of income is mass media–the business she has occupied herself with for over 25 years. Specializing in mass media, Oprah Winfrey runs daytime T.V. shows, Harpo Production Company and the Oprah Winfrey Learning Academy, making her one of the wealthiest black Americans in the world. Her current net worth stands at $3 billion.

Marsai Martin

Actress and Producer

Marsai Martin is an American teen actor and producer, best known for the popular comedy series 'Black-ish.' She was born in Little Elm, Texas, and began modeling when she was just a toddler. She was signed at the age of 5 and her first commercial was for 'Choice Hotels.' At 9 years old, her family moved to Los Angeles with her hoping to grab film and TV roles. Soon, she earned the first TV role of her career. She was cast as 'Diane Johnson,' one of the main characters on 'Black-ish" in all five seasons of the hit comedy series and was honored with several award nominations for her acting. She also played in films such as 'Nina' and 'Fun Mom Dinner.' Also, she has worked as an executive producer and played a key role in the film 'Little.' At the age of 13, she became the youngest person in Hollywood to produce a film.

Affiong L. Affiong

Political Activist and Organizer

Affiong was born in Lagos, Nigeria and is a pan-Africanist who advocates for African human rights. She does lectures around the world regarding social justice and the development of African people. She also supports women's rights and reparations. She is dedicated to the struggle for Pan African freedom, unification and self-determination.

Megan Pete

Activit and Entertainer

Stage Name Megan Thee Stallion

Megan Pete is known by her stage name, Megan Thee Stallion; however, the controversial artist in present-day is an American rapper and activist for the protection and liberation of black women. Megan became the first female rapper to be signed by the American record label *300 Entertainment* while being a college student. She came into the spotlight for the first time through social media. Megan Thee Stallion has used digital platforms to make her way to the mainstream music world. She has used the video and image sharing platform Instagram to promote her free-styling and free speech.

THE WOMEN WHO HELPED TO ADVANCE SCIENCE

3

History has had its impact on the lives of black people in the medical community in various ways. Black women and children were used for experimental purposes regularly and some survived, and others fell to their untimely demise. Due to these contributions of involuntarily experiments done on black people science would not have become what it is today.

Henrietta Lacks, The HeLa Cells

Lacks was born August 1, 1920 and died October 4, 1951. She was an African American woman whose cancer cells are the source of the HeLa cell line, the first immortalized human cell line, and one of the most important cell lines in medical research. An immortalized cell line reproduces indefinitely under specific conditions, and the HeLa cell line continues to be a source of invaluable medical data to the present day.

The Experiments

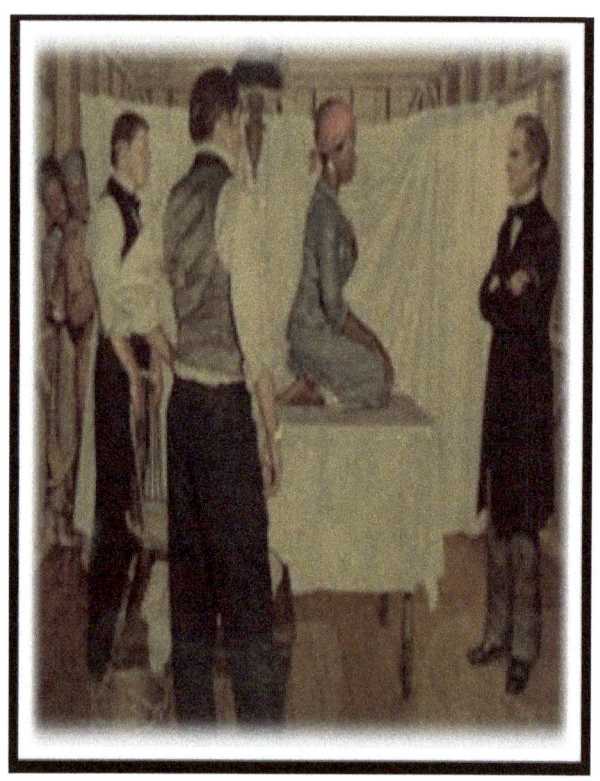

Many black women and children have contributed to science involuntarily. Many endured pain and torture, others disfigured but lived through it all, and many died. Because they were slaves, they had no civil or human rights, and many were used to advance science to where it is today. For instance, Physicians like James Marion Sims developed tools and surgical techniques related to women's reproductive health, known as the "father of modern gynecology." Sims did these experiments, cutting into the wombs of black women without anesthesia or medical ethicists. Because, like many others of that time, he did not believe these women would feel pain because they were black. Sims also experimented with newborn infants, who would not survive it.

Who is Sara Baartman 'Saartjie'?

Saartjie was born at the Gamtoos river in what is now known as the Eastern Cape. Her large buttocks and unusual color made her the object of fascination by the colonial Europeans, who presumed that they were racially superior. They wanted Sara to come to London as an oddity for display. She moved to London, where she was displayed "the ne plus ultra of hideousness" and "the greatest deformity in the world." People paid to see Sara's half-naked body showed in a cage that was about a meter and half high. She became an attraction for people from all over Europe. In 1814, she was transported from England to France and was nicknamed "Hottentot Venus," studied as a science specimen. Sara was used to help emphasize the stereotype that Africans were oversexed and a lesser race. Sara Baartman died at the age of 26. Her body was dismembered and kept in a museum for display until 2002. Her remains returned to Africa, where they were laid to rest.

ELOGEIA HADLEY

4

IN HONOR OF THE WOMEN, MEN AND CHILDREN THAT LOST THEIR LIVES TO LYNCHINGS

Our history contains several stories of triumph but unfortunately, it also contains sadness, injustice, and pain, many black people were lynched including women and children. Although many of their names are unknown these are a few of their stories. -

The Lynching of
Mary Turner

Mary Turner, 20 years old, was eight months pregnant at the time. Her husband had been one of several victims of "lynchings" on Sunday, May 19. Mary turner publicly objected to her husband's murder. She also dared to threaten to swear out warrants for those responsible. Those "unwise remarks," as the area papers put it, enraged locals. Mary Turner fled for her life, only to be caught and taken to Folsom's Bridge on the Brooks and Lowndes Counties' border. To punish her, at Folsom's Bridge, the mob tied Mary Turner by her ankles, hung her upside down from a tree, poured gasoline on her, and burned off her clothes. One member of the mob then cut her stomach open, and her unborn child dropped to the ground where it was reportedly stomped on and crushed by a member of the crowd, her body was then filled with bullets. Later that night, she and her baby were buried ten feet away from where they were both murdered. The makeshift grave was marked with only a "whiskey bottle" with a "cigar" stuffed in its neck.

Three days after the murder of Mary Turner and

her baby, three more bodies were found in the same area, including Sydney Johnson, who was killed in a shootout in Valdosta, Georgia. Once executed, the crowd of more than 700 people cut off his genitals and threw them into the street, A rope tied to his neck, and his body drug for nearly 20 miles to Morven, Georgia, 16 miles away and they burned his remains. Shortly after this chain of events, it is reported that more than 500 people fled Lowndes and Brooks Counties in fear for their lives.

The Story of "No Name"

The British merchants subjected millions of African people from the late 16th century to the 1830s to inhumane and brutal treatment. The example that brought the attention of the English abolitionist is the tale of John Kimber, a veteran of the slave trader who in 1791 skippered The Recovery of a 200-ton ship, from Bristol to the slaving coast of west Africa. Kimber's victim was a girl around 12 or 13 years of age. Since on the Recovery, the girl had been raped, brutalized and inflicted with gonorrhea and of course, she was the blame for the spread of the disease, not the British sailors. When the girl would not "dance" with the other enslaved Africans, Kimber flogged her with whips and ropes. Soon, she was struggling to walk, suffering from a bad leg. This was a problem for Kimber because if the girl is sick and damaged goods, she would get a much lower price when they ship docked at Grenada. Kimber's "solution" was brutal even by slaving standards. From the mizzenmast of the ship, he strung the girl up by her "bad" leg, then her other leg, and then by her arms. In each position, he whipped her. The ordeal lasted half an hour, after which the girl crawled to the hatch, fell, collapsed, convulsed and died. "The bitch is sulky," Kimber said. There is no record of her name, her story or her family and disturbingly, she is referred to as "No-name". After being denounced, Kimber was quickly brought up on charges of murder before the High Court of Admiralty, which was the only place to try a man for a crime on the high seas. After a short trial, John Kimber was acquitted of all charges.

Hanging of Celia

C elia was born in Missouri sometime during 1836; at 14 years old, she was purchased by Robert Newsom in 1850 after the death of Newsom's wife. He needed a female slave to serve as a cook for the household and to also fulfill his sexual needs. He turned to his fourteen-year-old slave after several rapes over years and she had also had 2 children by Newsom; other sources question the paternity of one of Celia's children as she had begun a romantic relationship with George, one of Newsom's other slaves, sometime before 1855. Celia and George had a consensual relationship, but throughout the relationship with George, she had to continually endure unwanted sexual advances from Robert Newsom. After enduring countless acts of abuse, Celia had finally had enough.

After some coaxing from new beau George, Celia was finally ready to take matters into her own hands. The sixty-year-old Newsom continued to rape Celia throughout this pregnancy. From Celia's account, she suffered from extreme morning sickness throughout her pregnancy and begged Newsom to leave her alone. Celia even went so far as to beg Virginia and Mary to talk to their father on her behalf but to no avail. Having started a relationship with Celia, George was furious that

Newsom continued to have a sexual relationship with his girlfriend. Later accounts record that George told his pregnant girlfriend, "He would have nothing more to do with her if she did not quit the old man."

Celia approached Robert Newsom on the morning of June 23, 1855, and told the old man that she would not take any more abuse and that she did not want to have a sexual relationship with him any longer. Of course, Newsom ignored Celia's warning and said, "He was coming to her cabin that night." Celia went looking for a weapon sometime on June 23. She found a large branch or stick on the property and carried it back to her cabin, placing it in the corner of her room. As promised, Robert Newsom entered Celia's cabin sometime that same night. The time had come, and Newsom entered her cabin on June 23 and began to make advances toward her. The pregnant woman grabbed the stick she had collected earlier as a warning; Newsom continued to make advancements. Celia then picked up the stick and gave Newsom a blow to the head. The initial hit angered him; Celia second blow to the head left Newsom dead on the cabin floor.

After killing Newsom, the pregnant 19 yr. old burned the body but had not burned it completely. She however continued burning the body well into the morning, but it was more than she could handle, so Celia recruited Newsom's grandson, to help dispose of the ash with promises to give him walnuts. unknowingly, He shoveled and laid the ashes along with the stables.

The morning came and Newsom's children began to look for him for hours. They began to suspect George, Celia's lover. He directed them to look closer to Newsom's home as a hint to find the suspect. They questioned Celia and she lied at first that she had not seen him but later confessed. The questions continued; several more hours had passed, and Celia stated the devil got into her as she repeated her story.

It was during the beginning of the civil war, her trial was delayed, but Celia was formally indicted by a grand jury. Judge William Augustus Hall appointed Celia her defense team led by John Jameson. Nearly two months later, as instructed, she entered a plea of "not guilty," and the trial officially began. On October 9, 1855, Celia was brought before a jury of twelve white men in the Callaway County Circuit Court.

On October 10, 1855, the jury found Celia guilty of murder in the first degree. At the time, Missouri law stated that it was a crime "to take any woman unlawfully against her will and by force, menace or duress, compel her to be defiled." The law also stated that resistance to this offense would give a justifiable excuse for a woman to murder a man.

Celia's defense team tried to use this strategy during the trial.

The defense argued that "any woman" should include enslaved women. However, this was unacceptable because a black slave woman was not seen as human in the eyes of the law. With the trial decided, Celia was found guilty of first-degree murder and was sentenced to death. Her defense team appealed the conviction but was denied by the Supreme Court of Missouri in December 1855. While waiting for her fate in the Callaway County jail around December, Celia gave birth to her third child. The baby, either fathered by Robert Newsom or George, was stillborn. Her other children were sold to Newsom's 2 sons. Celia was marched to the gallows at the age of nineteen. On December 21, 1855, Celia was hanged at 2:30 in the afternoon.

FOUR LITTLE GIRLS

On September 15, 1963, a bomb explodes during Sunday morning services in the 16th Street Baptist Church in Birmingham, Alabama, killing four young girls: The church bombing was the third in Birmingham in 11 days after a federal order came down to integrate Alabama's school system. Fifteen sticks of dynamite were planted in the church basement, underneath what turned out to be the girls' restroom. The bomb detonated at 10:19 a.m., killing Cynthia Wesley, Carole Robertson and Addie Mae Collins—all 14 years old—11-year-old Denise McNair, and many other church members were injured. Birmingham is a "symbol of hardcore resistance to integration." Alabama's governor, George Wallace, made preserving racial segregation one of the central goals of his administration, and Birmingham had one of the most violent chapters of the Ku Klux Klan. A well-known Klan member, Robert Chambliss, was charged with murder and buying 122 sticks of dynamite. And after FBI further investigation three other men assisted in the crime, Bobby Frank Cherry, Herman Cash and Thomas E. Blanton, Jr. Although in October 1963, Chambliss was cleared of the murder charge and received a six-month jail sentence and a $100 fine for the dynamite. Several years later in 1977, Chambliss was sentenced to life in prison, Herman Cash had already died and the remaining men who helped were also sentenced to life in 2000.

Lives Lost

As I come to the end of writing this book, we have had more challenges as a community and throughout the world. We have lost so many lives between police brutality, gang violence and a global pandemic that seemed to have chosen its victims, Black people! The statistics by the CDC suggestion Black people and the elderly are the hardest hit by this pandemic due to various reasons, because of underlying socioeconomic issues and underlying medical conditions. So, we must learn to take better care of ourselves. The black community seems to also be under siege; we are being murdered and killed by our own hands in our own communities with crime out of control.

I have found myself overwhelmed every time I hear of another black person being murdered in a country our ancestors work so hard to build and protect. it is hard to believe in the year 2020, we are still singing and praying to be saved and marching in protest to spare our lives. When will we understand the first law of nature is "self-preservation" and that we are supposed to do what it takes to stay alive? We cannot wait any longer for others to decide that our lives have value; we must do that for ourselves.

Say HER Name

There are many names of black women gone too soon. Black African women are also victims of police brutality and there is rarely any justice at all at the end. This is nothing new; it has been happening for years. Black women face trauma in their daily lives. We have watched our sons murdered and on tv, our children shot by police; we have seen our sisters pulled over for minor traffic violations and belittled, later to be found dead, and killed while sleeping in their own beds. Time and time again, there is no justice; only to understand this system was not built for the slaves or their descendants. However, it is time for that to change; it is time for justice! R.I.P.

'Still I Rise' by Maya Angelou

You may write me down in history
With your bitter, twisted lies,
You may trod me in the very dirt
But still, like dust, I'll rise.

Does my sassiness upset you?
Why are you beset with gloom?
'Cause I walk like I've got oil wells
Pumping in my living room.

Just like moons and like suns,
With the certainty of tides,
Just like hopes springing high,
Still I'll rise.

Did you want to see me broken?
Bowed head and lowered eyes?
Shoulders falling down like teardrops.
Weakened by my soulful cries.

Does my haughtiness offend you?
Don't you take it awful hard
'Cause I laugh like I've got golden mines
Diggin' in my own back yard.

ELOGEIA HADLEY

You may shoot me with your words,
You may cut me with your eyes,
You may kill me with your hatefulness,
But still, like air, I'll rise.

Does my sexiness upset you?
Does it come as a surprise
That I dance like I've got diamonds
At the meeting on my thighs?

Out of the huts of history's shame
I rise
Up from a past that's rooted in pain
I rise
I'm a black ocean, leaping and wide,
Welling and swelling I bear in the tide.
Leaving behind nights of terror and fear
I rise
Into a daybreak that's wondrously clear
I rise
Bringing the gifts that my ancestors gave,
I am the dream and the hope of the slave.
I rise
I rise
I rise.

Our MISSING and EXPLOITED

E very day black women and children go missing, not just in the United States, but all over the world. Many believe this is due to sex trafficking, while some are being taken for other reasons. Recent studies have shown that black women and children go missing more often than white women and children. According to the National Center for Missing and Exploited

Children, of the estimated 613,000 people reported missing in the U.S., about 60%, majority of that percentage are black. Although black women make up less than 7% of the U.S. population, they represent about 10% of all missing person cases throughout the country. Estimates by the Black and Missing Foundation put the total number of disappeared black women and girls at 64,000 yearly. Unfortunately, black, missing women and girls are rarely looked for, because they are often classified as runaways rather than missing persons, shifting the focus from public safety to personal responsibility, making the victim at fault. According to Black and Missing's stereotypes about African Americans, crime also plays a role in the inconsistency in media coverage. Black people are often labeled as criminal associates, involved with drugs and gangs, or assumed to live in areas where crime is a part of their daily lives. Law enforcement officials and government and community leaders have said media coverage does not reflect that reality and media and officials does not assist in finding them. Some of our missing sisters and children have made their way home and were found in some instances by family and neighbors coming together to search for their own. And the reality is, many will never be seen again.

5

TIGNON LAWS

Regulating the appearance of black women

I s a tignon or a headdress\head wrap used to cover hair? It was worn by free and slave Creole women of African ancestry in Louisiana in 1786. Governor Esteban Rodriguez Miró enacted the law that was supposed to regulate black women's hairstyles. Black women's features often attracted male white men, and their beauty was a threat to white women. The tignon law was to prevent white men from pursuing Creole women who passed for white because these black women competed too openly with white women by dressing elegantly, but black women did not anguish. Instead, they abided by the rules and did what black women do today; they turned it into fashion. They changed the laws to demean, but the black woman took it and made it work for them. The women used unique colors, jewels, ribbons and wrapping styles, which accentuated their elegance even more. Black women have worn head coverings in the Caribbean islands, Guadeloupe and Dominica, which included hidden messages. They used popular fabric amongst slaves. Even as the laws ended in the 1800s, black women worldwide still wrap their hair for protective styles and as an accessory.

6

The Code Switch

ELOGEIA HADLEY

Being a black woman is a challenge, especially if you love your natural self; it is also problematic to wear your natural hair and be yourself. Before slavery, black people were told they were ugly and uncivilized, and our skin tone was considered unacceptable, even offensive.

In many countries, there were laws and policies written to prevent us from being our natural selves. It was something about our hair that made Europeans feel uncomfortable and you know, that was not allowed. We were to make sure they were always comfortable. There was a point in history when Europeans would breed out the dark melanin by mating a dark person with a white European and after the experiment was over, they recognized within a few generations the melanin would eventually disappear. Even now, to be accepted in some areas you must have straighter hair "good hair", long narrow noses and be lighter-skinned. We have been forced to conform to

European standards of beauty, even though the African is the first on the planet with organic beauty and original features. The Africans were the first with blonde hair and blue eyes, and everything in between, but we were forced to adapt in this society and to live without incident or punishment; we had to become someone else esthetically, emotionally, physically as well as mentally when not around friends and family or in our community; this is called "the code switch". Who we are in our homes and our private circles, are not who we are at work or school. When we are outside our comfort zones, we must walk, talk and behave in a certain manner so that we do not offend white people. and so on.

Many black women wear wigs and weave because our natural hair is seen as unkept or unclean and not accepted by society. History has proven African women invented wigs, extensions and weaves as an accessory for beauty; this was hundreds of years before African colonization. African standards of beauty had no other standards to compare it to. It was only the African, whether it was the sophistication of Egypt (Kemet) or the raw natural beauty of the Zulu in South Africa. Africans have beauty like no other ethnic group on the planet, but nowadays, many wear wigs and lace front weaves to hide their true selves to satisfy the status quo.

Yet, we do what we must do to survive, we walk straight ahead without our natural sway to avoid attention; we are forced to speak "Proper English" or be misunderstood or called unapproachable. As Black women, we sacrifice who we are to make sure we are not dismissed from our jobs and are accepted.

We must pretend to be someone else to get us through our day-to-day lives and we have done it so long, we turned against ourselves and became that fake persona; some of us have gone as far as surgery or bleaching. When we do this, we become invisible, telling ourselves that being who we are naturally is not good enough. And the sad part is, we passed this down to our children; we gave them identity issues, we place in them a self-hate that you can see from the smallest black child. We see black people bleaching their skin and wearing what I call permanent weaves and wigs to be 'beautiful'. These are hairpieces that seem to never come off and some women have not seen their natural hair for months at a time on purpose. The things we do to be accepted are not worth it in the end; after we do all of this, we are still not accepted, and in the process, we lose ourselves. I decided that I am who I am. I am going to walk my walk and talk my talk, wear my hair how I want and feel beautiful. I am teaching my children to do the same. Wear your crown!

ELOGEIA HADLEY

"The most disrespected person in America is the black woman, The most unprotected person in America is the black woman, The most neglected person in America is- the black woman."

-Malcolm X

Candid
Conversations
Sistah 2 Sistah

As black women we need to talk, we should have more conversations as sisters in a safe place where we can vent. Because we have more in common than differences, we need sister circles all over the world to support and build a sisterhood. These are some of the conversations we should have.

Black Women Being Angry, is it a "MYTH?"

B lack women are the strongest on the planet; we have proven this to be true. If not, tell me a stronger woman. We are strong because of what we have endured and accomplished despite our trials and tribulations, and because of this, black women should not be compared to any other woman. There is no other woman like a black woman, no story or journey more complicated than that of the black African woman.

Our passion for things may seem overwhelming to watch, and for others who do not understand us or our culture, they misconstrued what they see as anger. They say we are too loud and too opinionated or overbearing. Because of many misconceptions of who they think the black woman is, she is usually demonized by society and the media. There is a misunderstanding regarding black women, and sometimes she does not even understand the power that she possesses. She has overcome so much, just like her mother. She learned to balance what life throws at her, even the things that never belonged to her; she carried it all and still stood firm.

ELOGEIA HADLEY

The black woman has worked in the fields from sunup to sundown. She had her children taken from her and sold off, and yet, nursed children that weren't hers. She was also a healer, a midwife and it seemed there was nothing she couldn't do.

She was the woman who pulled our men off those hanging trees and tended the wounds of the battered and broken, the same women that stood next to our men in the picket lines, voting lines and fought off dogs, then went home and cooked meals and raised our children with no sweat. Black women support many while her pains are ignored; she still woke up the next day renewed and ready for what the world was going to throw at her, and she made this look easy.

She was called ugly, nappy-headed and told that nothing about her was desirable, yet the slave masters laid with her and bore several children from her womb, not from love, but desire. Being afraid of her God-given beauty, she hid the best parts of her in shame. Black women made a way out of no way. Forced to eat what was leftover, she made it work, and it made her strong. When food was scarce, she planted and picked greens, weeds and used herbs, making something of it that nourished her body and soul.

She has stood the test of time abused, mistreated, abandoned, raped, ignored, fondled and called ugly, used as Guinea pigs for science and sexual exploitation. As unloved as she is, what woman has endured so much and yet continues daily? Instead of asking her why she was so loud? You should stop and listen to her screams, instead of saying she is angry; ask her about her passions, instead of hurting and abandoning her, stand beside her and be her shoulder; instead of watching her fall, find ways to pick her up. Her loyalty will go unmatched by you. Moreover, when they ask the questions why does she get an "Attitude?", why is she so "Angry? " Why is she not smiling? Listen to her and give her a reason to smile.

Many times, what others see is a strength, endurance, and confidence they do not understand, cannot relate to and may not even possess themselves. In many ways, what you see are angry black women in pain. Many mask pains in many ways, and there are consequences for hundreds of years and generations after generations of abuse. After a while, you stop hoping, and you lose faith, but we do not understand how to give up or how to stop. We keep going and remain standing and looking for happiness despite the hard and uneven road beneath our feet. It is hard to smile when you have been disappointed time after time. She is not angry she is fed up, and the fiercest warrior needs a break.

I Am Not Your Super Woman

"Just learn to let go, take off your cape and BREATHE!"

The pain that black women have endured over hundreds of years has made many of us hard and rough around the edges. It is in our blood to withstand the worst of it and still pretend to be unbothered by the bumps and scratches in this stressful life, but we have learned to work around it, at least look the part. It is time black women stepped back and took a breath.

Amid the mayhem, we go from one trauma to another, holding back tears appearing to be tough, not allowing anyone to help us because we don't want to look weak and show we are vessels damaged and nearly broken. So we hold our head up put a happy face, a mask for the world. We have held our breath for far too long; it's time for us to breathe and allow others to help us because we have done the work, we have been loyal to others but not to ourselves, we have been the strong one and we have cried behind closed doors far too many times.

We pretend that we do not need anyone or anything to help us, but we do and always have. There is nothing wrong with not being the strongest ones. It's time to allow others to stand on their own so we can unbend our backs, stand up straight and finally breathe. It is not weak to know when to let go and allow your vulnerability to show a little. What does that make you? Human! And you cannot save the world if you cannot first save yourself. Just learn to let go, take off your cape and BREATHE!

I am A Strong Black Woman, and I Don't Need No Man!

Does this way of thinking lead to loneliness and bitterness, when we hear this phrase from black women? What does this mean? Is she saying, literally "she doesn't need a man" or "she doesn't need anybody"? Black women are typically not allowed to feel vulnerable or have moments of weakness, but we must admit that they are exhausted doing it all alone, being convinced to do all, be-all, all the time to everybody.

Some black women have gotten to the point they are bitter and beyond repair, and many are doing the best they can. As a black woman, I have never said, "I don't need a man" because, in all actuality, I do. Not need, but want a companion for love and life, and I know this is not true for some because of abuse they have received from some black men Whatever her reasons are, some black women are so bitter they don't trust others around them; this is how they protect their hearts and souls from any further damage.

Many black women put up the wall so high and so deep, you can't dig under or fly over it, and they burn the bridge of return as well. Some say they don't care and that they are OK with it all, so they put on an act saying to themselves 'it's not that bad', but that is a lie you can almost see in their eyes, the pain of having no one to help and support them daily with the children, the house and the finances. I know it's complicated.

We all need someone, especially during lonely nights. I know some wish they had someone at night to satisfy them sexually or just someone to share their time with, but I understand the pain and the mental anguish they are trying to avoid by remaining single and independent. It is unfortunate, because they are alienating them-selves from possible love.

Many black women had men in their lives that were not abusive and did not victimize them, and we can't blame all men because of the few bad ones we have encountered. However, when you see examples of positive black men around you, i.e., your fathers, grandfathers, brothers or cousins, you tend to have a better outlook on relationships, and you will teach your sons differently because of the examples you saw.

Some black women are so severely damaged that they have put up a persona to hide the fact they are hurt. "I do not need a man" may mean "I can do it alone, and I do not need you!" They are not saying they don't need anyone. They are having a hard time and don't want you to add on to it. That's why you hear them say, "I can do bad by myself," and many cannot find a man willing to contribute to their lifestyle. I also know some black women are OK with who they are and where they are in life, and they are not ready to change a thing for a man or anyone else.

We must realize that both black women and black men are damaged, and most of our issues came from outside of our communities. We had systematic racism and social engineering that always interfered with our lives. The war on black communities is real. This system wants the black women weak, alone and bitter and to do this, you have to hurt her to the point she has to blame someone, and it's usually the black man. She is not going to blame herself; she needs to point the finger at her pain, and it's him, he did it! We must admit, it is not all him... he is not always wrong, and you are not always right. There was a time we were cordial and respectful to one another.

We must remember it was not always this way;

only 65 years ago, black people had their communities, married, raised black children and if there was a struggle, they did it together. We must ask ourselves what happened to know why black women are the most unmarried woman according to some statistics at over 50%. That is a big jump in such a short time, and where do we go from here? What do we have to do to build better relationships with each other? So black women need the black man. We need each other. Facing some realities and asking ourselves these questions will begin to put our communities back together again.

The Good Black Woman?

During all the issues within ourselves, all the responsibilities, many lost themselves. We are not the same women we used to be; each generation of women is different from the next for obvious reasons. Nevertheless, whatever they went through, they knew they needed their community, and the men and women needed each other. They knew that was the glue that held the community together.

We are also a new breed of women, we are more independent and that's not all bad, but we are also more masculine today. So I ask the question, 'are we losing our femininity?' Or is this who we have always been? I have noticed we walk, talk and "Act" like men more than ever and I believe our natural balance is off, because we have had to do everything such as work, provide and be breadwinners, etc.

It is a historical fact that black women have never been weak, fragile or docile, because we come from warriors and female kings, even then we remained healers, nurturers, mothers and lovers; and our men honored us for it. Now in this patriarchal religious society, we are taught we have a role to play and for women, we are to be the "submissive" ones. For the ancient African community, being submissive was not a thing; there was nothing wrong with a woman leading and the man following, because she was seen as an equal. Now, our feminity is being challenged and misconstrued because we don't fit in this role invented by Eurocentric biblical ideologies.

What we need is to restore our natural balance and accept one another for who we are and what we provide for each other and the community. It is ok to be vulnerable with one another; expressing our femininity is powerful. It is your softer side. It's when you allow yourself to open up and be vulnerable and that's ok. At the same time, you can still be independent because one has nothing to do with the other. My grandmother used to say, "you can get more with honey"; that meant to be nice and you will get a better reaction that may lead to benefits.

I am not saying to be weak or play the damsel in

distress. I am only saying the balance should be restored, the masculine and femininity energies need each other to balance. Sometimes it is about feeding the ego. Masculine energy wants to be needed and useful and when they are not, they wonder "what does she need me for"? "How am I useful to her"? some of us have lost our way because we do not have any examples of what balance looks like in a relationship anymore. So there is confusion on both sides.

Here are a few suggestions I thought that may help with balancing our feminine and masculine energy and what being a good woman may look like.

As a good woman, a good person, we should be an ear and a shoulder for each other because the world is hateful and mean enough to black people. Some men are not religious and still will see Jesus as another man who is getting credit for what he has done in the home. Many of our men do not want to hear 'thank you, Jesus', after he has worked hard all day to pay the bills and provide. Thank your man first, if that is what he requires.

Remember, black men have feelings too. They're not robots; be more intune to how you treat one another, especially around other people, and do not belittle him to prove a point. Sit down and talk; put the cell phones down, no friends or family around, no children in the room, and just talk about life, what's happening in the world, what is best for the children and how to keep your sanity living in this world.

Meditate, pray, hold hands and hug more; a little affection goes a long way. Try to understand that it is you both against the world, and the war is outside, so do not bring the war inside your home. Let there be peace and balance where you lay your head, especially with each other.

Does Black Love Exist?

I have had several conversations with many black women who are single, looking for love and waiting for someone to sweep them off their tired feet. Many go as far as meeting on social media, dating sites and some have decided to take whatever is available and deal with the drama, or date outside of their blackness, all out of desperation, just plain tired and lonely, and who wants to be alone forever? Many want it all-the husband, children, dog and white picket fence, but some of us may just want the wedding bells and whistles, but not the responsibility of marriage. Really ask yourself, are you ready to commit your time, effort and life to another human being? Marriage is like a business, two people who give up their sole proprietorship to become incorporated; both parties have to be in this agreement 100% or it won't work.

Many black women wanted to do things the right way, get an education, start a career, get married you know "the right way"; but the way things are, it seems the right way is an unreachable dream. I wanted to offer suggestions and hope. Black love does exist, but black women would have to go outside of their comfort zone and themselves to look at them instead of local love. Love may be in

South Africa, Brazil or Jamaica and yes, you might have to relocate or bring them to you, which I recommend, but be careful to do some background checks; talk to family and friends, if possible. We must keep ourselves safe at all costs. What chances are you willing to take to find black love and get out of the house? Start volunteering at hospitals, churches, children's homes etc. Make yourself available; at the same time, you are helping the community. This way, maybe black love will find you.

After talking to black men about dating black women, many black men want to have a real conversation with a black woman about life, struggles and goals. Black men said let's talk about something else besides, what kind of car I drive, and they want to also see us go back to our natural selves.

We as black people must understand how

important black men and women loving each other is; black love is the key to overcoming diversity and promoting structure and stability. So, we black people must teach black love to our children so it won't seem so foreign to them. This way, when they are adults, they will seek to have a black family and build strong black communities. One takeaway for my Sista's is LOVE YOU FIRST, self-love is the first romance, even if you don't find the black knight in shining armor. But I pray love finds you!

Raising Black Children

As mothers, we are the first teacher of the children. They begin learning in our wombs, listening to our language, our tone of voice and sharing our nutrients. As the first teachers, you are responsible for giving them all the tools they need to progress in life, especially if you are raising the children alone, it is crucial what you teach them. As black women, we must educate our children about things white women do not have to. I have found we need to teach our children how to be safe being black in this world. For instance, we must teach our children how to carry themselves to avoid being victimized, how to avoid trouble while being black, what to do if they have a police run-in, how to react to racism and how to love themselves completely. We should stop lying to our children about the world. They need to know what we are dealing with living in a black body and how to navigate outside our black space. We are not protecting them by lying to them as if everything is OK. It is NOT! It just makes things harder to understand later in their lives. We could just make things simple and direct. These are a few suggestions:

- Be honest with your children about life.
- Teach responsibility and accountability, especially about sex.
- Teach good hygiene.

- Teach them self-care and how important it is to take care of their bodies.
- Teach simple economic. How to save money and practice good spending habits.
- Teach them to respect themselves and others.
- Teach them to use logic and not emotions to make decisions. Think first!
- Try not to spoil them by giving them everything because the world won't.
- Teach them to earn what they want because nothing is given to them for free.
- Teach them the importance of self-love. Our children need to love themselves before they can love anyone or anything else.

I am not trying to change the way you educate your children, but I have observed our children, and something is wrong, and we must change it. As mothers to our sons, we need to make sure that they will be able to navigate this planet without incident. Sadly, our sons have targets on their backs, and our children are not seen as children. Studies have shown that black children are generally mistaken as adults and treated as such. So, it is up to us to love and nurture our seeds, so they can survive and get all they need to grow.

Is It OK to Be Vulnerable?

Is it time for Black women to admit that they are vulnerable, unhealthy and doing it all alone? We must realize it is time to ask for and accept help from others. It's not a weakness to need someone, because everybody needs somebody, especially in hard times, whether it be family or friends; you do not have to do it alone. As black women, we must give ourselves credit for holding it all together - life, work and children. We have been through the worst of any other women on the planet, and we are still standing, but there is a point when you can say I need help; I am tired of doing it alone. Just say, "HELP ME."

What Do Black Men Think?

I asked black men these Questions:

What do you think about BLACK WOMEN? What would you like to say to BLACK WOMEN?

1. "Black women are letting themselves go (gaining too much weight) and need to take better care of themselves."
2. "Black women are no fun to be around."
3. "Black women like to argue too much. And always seem to be looking for an argument."
4. "Black women never seem happy or appreciate what you do for them."
5. "Black women never take responsibility for the part they did wrong."
6. "Black women have become too shallow."
7. "Black women want something from black men that they do not have themselves."
8. "Black women should not blame all black men for what one black man did to them."
9. Be more proactive in the community speak out against the atrocities that are detrimental to our growth as a united people. I wish black women would be more involved in the community.

10. "Black single women should do a better job at raising their children?"
11. BE YO SELF the Godley woman yall are.
12. Be more proactive in the community speak out against the atrocities that are detrimental to our growth as a united people.
13. You guys are the most unappreciated women on the planet, I just want to say the world is nothing without yall, I love yall to life!
14. You are the most beautiful women on the planet earth. Act like it!
15. We love you!
16. Let us start by appreciating each other, and even that will take some doing, I guess it's an individual case by case.
17. That no matter our trials and tribulations, you are all we have.
18. Why do you wear weaves and wigs to look nice, you are already beautiful how you are.
19. Do not give up on us. Many of us are waking up, trying to be there for you the way you have been for us since the boats pulled into port.

Baggage

The bag Lady

W e all carry mental or emotional scars; we all have had trauma in our lives. It's the secrets that hurt us the most; they cut deep. There are so many levels of pain that we hold on to, but at what point do we let it all go? If we, don't it will keep us from elevating to our best self and affect the people around us, it's like poison. We must confront or let it go, so that we can be who we were born to be and live beyond and despite the pain, and if needed, get help. We owe it to ourselves not to let the past or people keep us from living our best life or walking in our purpose. Drop those bags and run!

MENTAL HEALTH

As black women, we do so much daily because we do not have a choice. Many of us take trauma and pass it down to our children through our DNA. Some studies have shown we are experiencing injuries our ancestors suffered years ago and we carry this trauma through the next generation. We are our ancestors, and in some ways, we must break the cycle. The only way to do that is to recognize the issues and deal with them accordingly. We have genetic PTSD (post-traumatic stress disorder). Dr. Joy Degruy did more studies specifically for African descendants here in America, and she found in her research that we continue the trauma from slavery. We respond and react the same way our ancestors did during that time, she calls it post-traumatic slave syndrome. This trauma of abuse, mistreatment and murder was never dealt with or ever healed on any level. In our community, we learn to just deal with it, ignore it, avoid it and don't tell anyone else, or risk seeming weak. We think they may use our pain against us. A quote by Dr. joy Degruy says, "It's the secrets that kill us." Black women have been dying inside for years carrying secrets of being molested, abused, mistreated and abandoned. There was a time we had each other tell our deepest darkest secrets. This new black woman talks less and will not share her pain with anybody. She instead self-destructs for fear of judgment. We used the church to shout it out, the beauty shops to talk it out, we would sit around the kitchen table Sunday morning getting our hair pressed, we talked about what was happening in our lives. We bonded over food at the dinner table. We had places where we were accepted and protected. Now we have no sacred spaces, not even to vent the frustrations of our daily lives. I am a success story of the pain of my rape or molestation because I decided to do something about it. I looked within and knew I could not allow my past to occupy space in my soul, so I let go, and with the help of therapy and my ancestors, I stop keeping secrets and let the chips fall where they may. If someone mistreated you, try not to bring your baggage into your current relationship; it is venom. It will kill the life of your relationships and your marriage.

We are all damaged, but if you cannot seem to get over your past and move on, you cannot function with anger, resentment, hatred and regrets. You should think about getting psychological help to bring peace to your mind and soul.

OUR HEALTH AND WELLNESS!

Our health is essential, and we must take care of ourselves, otherwise, we cannot take care of anyone else. We suffer many ailments in our community from high blood pressure, diabetes and cancers. We should do the best we can in preventing diseases.

Here are some basic tips for staying healthy.

1. Bathe often and use natural gentle soaps and oils.
2. Wash your hair depending on the hairstyle if you wear weaves, braids and wigs wash, condition, and keep the oils in your hair.
3. Brush and floss teeth in the morning and after heavy meals and desserts.
4. Stay hydrated drink plenty of water per day.
5. Keep your skin soft by using natural oils and lotions with less alcohol or chemicals.

6. Let you diet consist of more vegetables and fruit, then processed and junk foods.
7. Get a physical with complete blood work every 9-12 months more if you have conditions to be monitored.
8. See a gynecologist and do daily breast exams.
9. Avoid stress and drama as much as possible.
10. Exercise daily at least 30 minutes per day 3 to 4 times per week. That includes walking or dancing.
11. Meditate at least 5 minutes per day. It will help with stress.
12. We are missing many nutrients and vitamins in our daily diets. If possible, eating plenty of green vegetables make fresh vegetable juices and smoothies as a meal replacement.
13. Detox often: in a glass container of distilled or spring water, and add chopped cucumber, a lime, or lemon, thumb size ginger, and mint leaves for taste.
14. You should ask your physician to check your vitamin levels, especially vitamin D and Iron. Because we do not get enough sunlight or enough iron in our food, and we

also loose blood during our periods. And for healthy skin, nails and hair, we may need to replace several vitamins. Many of us suffer from alopecia, dry skin, and brittle nails die of vitamin deficiency.

Iron	Iodine
Vitamin D	Vitamin B
Calcium	Vitamin A
Magnesium	Fiber
Folic acid	Omega 3 oils

In many cases, probiotics and prebiotics are needed to balance good and bad bacteria in the stomach, and there is sea moss that contains many vitamins we need all at once.

Your Spiritual Connection!

The African woman has always been the most spiritual person on the planet. She was there at the very beginning of it all as the healer, even in the darkest times. She found the light and brought others out of the dark.

There was a time she would just walk out to her garden and cure you of whatever ailed you, she knew what herbs to use to restore. The African woman was a local doctor, nurse, medicine woman, shaman and midwife. She was nature, so she understood what to use to heal your mind, body and soul. She was at peace with life. She was appreciated and worshipped because of her spiritual guidance and healing abilities. Black women need to get back to their spiritual connections. Black women are the first made in the image of God herself!

"When all the women begin to go by their own physicians and heal themselves, whether it be at heart level, or a physical level. When she begins to do all her healing work, then she will be able to resurrect her family and be the medicine woman within her family."

-Queen Afua

ELOGEIA HADLEY

Money

Management

S o l u t i o n s !

Most of our money troubles come from never understanding economics and not being financially literate. We live from day to day, paycheck to paycheck just getting by. We spend it just as fast as we receive it. Some of us don't have a life insurance policy, or money set aside for an emergency. Because of our history, in general, we don't trust banks and may feel in many ways, we don't think about tomorrow when we can live today. Unfortunately, for our children, this is the wrong way to think; many of us die and leave our loved one's poor, in debt, confused and unsure what to do next. Some resort to borrowing money or starting a go-fund-me. Many were unable to pass down generational wealth, is this a generational curse or just a fear of succeeding? In our history, there were times black people-built businesses. Just imagine being a black person living in Tulsa, Oklahoma, Greenwood district called "Black Wall Street "in the early 1900s. Ex-slaves build that town brick by brick with their bare hands, and one day, it was all gone, burned down.

Many still carry that fear of building and saving for a future for fear someone will take it all away. So now, we earn money and spend it as soon as we get it with no savings. We must move beyond this and teach our next generation how to do better.

It is essential for black women, especially those

who are the head of households and bear the brunt of financial responsibility for their future and their children. We are getting sicker faster and more often than our white counterparts. We need rainy day money, life insurance, education about C.D.s, how to invest and build for not just us, for our future generations. We should be leaving benefits and not bills.

Money Management Tips

Tip 1 get an app that works for you to help manage your money

Tip 2 track what you spend habits

Tips 3 learn to use coupons

Tip 4 utilize your reward programs via grocery store or credit cards

Tip 5 utilizes your recurring transfer from your back from checking to savings

Tip 6 try a savings plan strategy

Tip 7 check out cashback programs

Tip 8 pay yourself first

Tip 9 Make your lunch

Tip 10 put all your bills on your credit card or auto pay from your account

Tip 11 use tracking apps

Tip 12 budget for more than your bills

Tip 13 thrift stores and clearance racks for clothes and shoes

Tip 14 cook more at home eating out is expensive

Tip 15 go back to the basic don't need name brands or costly items

Tip 16 decide with your recurring bills like car note insurance mortgage

Tip 17 always shop around for better deals for insurance, tv cables, and cell phone packages

Tip 18 never allow anyone to automatic debit your account agree to send it from your account to them

Tip 19 to save in gas walk, bike, rideshare, or transit if possible

Tip 20 stays on your path, change what needs to be changed but stay on your financial track

"Black women have faced systemic racism and sexism, along with unfair federal policies that have prevented us from obtaining quality housing, supporting our families, and creating long-term financial plans."

-Cameron Glover Quote from Refinery 29 April 10, 2017

ELOGEIA HADLEY

Entrepreneurship

Recent statics report that Black women are now the most educated women in the world, but why do it all, only to work for someone else? We must begin to use that education to build our businesses and work for ourselves. We should teach our young black daughters to do more than just go to school to get a job. They need to have a plan to avoid getting huge loans that will take years to pay back. Let that time you use getting A degrees work for you - pay off by being your boss. We also need to choose better majors in college. We should also take advantage of certificate programs because we are not all prepared for four years of university. As we know, black women are the most educated women in the world right now. We are also women in debt. Let's not get a master's degree only to brag, then struggle to pay back. I have heard women say, "get you a sugar daddy to take care of you because we are so overwhelmed". I hope women are not doing that for a designer bag. This is not cute; this can ruin reputations and self-esteem. We need to stop telling our girls that money only comes from men; teach them to get their own money, encourage self-love and entrepreneurship.

There is a whole generation looking up to Cardi B and Blac Chyna as role models. Certainly, no judgment. Although they are successful women, and they earned success with their bodies, it won't work for everyone. Let's begin to teach our daughters more than "sex equals money". Let us teach 'Real Estate equals money'; 'investing equals money' and 'using your intellect will keep your money'. There are other ways to get your money than overly exploiting and sexualizing ourselves; there will be the day that age will catch up to every young girl and that method of making money will no longer get them by. Let us ask ourselves. 'What is it all worth?'

ELOGEIAL HADLEY

The Fountain
of Youth

Melanin is why Black Don't Crack!

ELOGEIA HADLEY

Black women are admired for their youthful looks, naturally curly hair and ageless skin. Some women have cosmetic surgery and obtain melanin injections to achieve the look of black women. It is not by accident. Black women were born with it, and the secret is "Melanin." The pineal gland produces Melanin, shaped like a pinecone located in the brain. Many called it carbon or dark matter. Melanin has been studied for over 65 years by scientists because of its importance. Melanin is the reason black people walk, talk, dance and move differently than other people. Melanin covers the embryo after conception. Melanin is in all skin, hair, eyes, organs, blood and cells. It also protects from hot temperatures, and with Melanin, you age slower than people without it.

Other facts about Melanin:

- It takes melanin years to decay after death.
- Melanin reacts to sound and gravity.
- Melanin absorbs all energy, including the sun, and will attach itself to certain chemicals,
- Melanin is the most studied discover in the current science world since the Vietnam war when it was found that the black soldiers even after death, the pineal gland was still active. In contrast, most of the white soldiers had already calcified.
- The more Melanin you have, the more civilized you are, the more psychic you are, the more information you can store in your memory, the faster your nerve transmissions, the more you can absorb the full-spectrum sound, color, taste, smell, and touch.
- Melanin is why we run faster, jump higher, and more spiritual. Melanin can be considered the key to life.
- The best way to care for your Melanin is natural vitamins D (the sun) and drink water and eat plenty of vegetables daily.

- Your Melanin is precious and worth more gold literally. Melanin is worth over $380 a gram more than gold. To understand Melanin is to understand,

MELANIN IS THE KEY TO ALL LIFE!

12

My Message to Black Women

Black women have made significant contributions to the world from building nations to giving birth to them. So, we must understand we do not only represent ourselves. We are representing all of those that came before us. All the women that fought and died, healed, loved and nurtured generations, we must set an example for the young women coming after us. We must know that we are not our legs and thighs, breasts and back sides. We are so much more. We give birth to nations, and our womb is valuable. We can trace our mothers to the very beginning;

we are the ancient ones, so are our wombs. We should celebrate by taking better care of ourselves, loving ourselves unconditionally, loving each other and making sure the next generation loves themselves just as much. We are some of the most beautiful creatures on this planet. The first womb-man, and whether we are a dark chocolate mocha mix or caramel vanilla latte complexion, whether you have 4c kinky hair to the curliest curls or bone straight, we must know that we are beautiful, and we set the trend for beauty. Love and respect yourself, we are the Mothers of the universe. Goddess on the Rise!

"Dipped in chocolate, bronzed in elegance, enameled with grace, toasted in with beauty, my lord, she's a black woman."
-Dr. Yosef Ben Jochannan

ELOGEIA HADLEY

References & Definitions

13

LINKS AND WEBSITES

Pictures by the following websites and by google images.

By Encyclopedia Britannica, The editors of Encyclopedia Britannica, **Lucy**, May 15, 2013, https://www.britannica.com/topic/Lucy-fossil

By Erica Taylor, **The Ivory Bangle Lady**, Blackamericaweb.com, https://blackamericaweb.com/2011/05/09/the-ivory-bangle-lady/

By Ro Ho, Original People.Org, First Americans were Black according to BBC documentary,

ELOGEIA HADLEY

November 15, https://originalpeople.org/first-americans-were-black-aborigines-2/

By Sola Rey, found in a Brazilian cave "**The Luzia Woman**" is 11,500 years old, July 18, 2016, solarey.net/found-in-a-brazilian-cave-the-luzia-woman-is-11500-years-old/

By Newafrikan77, **Scientists Reveal That The Black Woman is The Mother of Humankind (Mitochondrial Eve /Mothers).**, January 11, 2017, https://newafrikan77.wordpress.com/2017/01/11/january-1988-scientists-reveal-that-the-black-woman-is-the-mother-of-humankind-mitochondrial-eve-mothers/

By Cheryle Moses First Humans: Mitochondrial Eve and Homo Sapiens in Africa's Great Rift Valley November 1, 2017 - https://blackgwinnett.com/black-pride/mitochondrial-eve-and-homo-sapiens-in-africas-great-rift-valley/

By Tseday, Posted in African History, Tagged with Blue Nile**, Cradle of Humanity**, East African Rift valley, Ethiopia, Lake, September 1, 2008, https://tseday.wordpress.com/2008/09/01/ethiopia-the-cradle-of-humanity/

By The Outpost, **Jean Jacques Dessalines and the Women Warriors who Liberated Haiti**, – Posted on January 24, 2018, https://Humanitywilderutopia.com/international/humanity/jean-jacques-dessalines-and-the-women-warriors-who-liberated-haiti/

By Collier Meyerson, Glamour, **Women of the Year, The Founders of Black Lives Matter**: "We Gave Tongue To Something That We All Knew Was Happening," November 1, 2016, https://www.glamour.com/story/women-of-the-year-black-lives-matter-founders

Miriam Makeba, WRITTEN BY DATE PUBLISHED, November 06, 2020 The Editors of Encyclopedia Britannicahttps://www.britannica.com/biography/Miriam-Makeba

ELOGEIA HADLEY

By PBS Finding Your Roots, Henry Louis Gates, **Lupita Nyongo' o**, Clip Season 4, Episode 7, Children of the Revolution, Premiered Tue, November 14, 2017, facebook.com/LupitaNyongo/videos/1523415411073687/
https://www.pbs.org/weta/finding-your-roots/watch/episodes/children-of-the-revolution

The famous people, **marsi martin**
https://www.thefamouspeople.com/profiles/marsai-martin-45004.php

By DeNeen L. Brown, Retropolis, **A surgeon experimented on slave women without anesthesia**. Now his statues are under attack.
URLhttps://washingtonpost.com/news/retropolis/wp/2017/08/29/a-surgeon-experimented-on-slave-women-without-anesthesia-now-his-statues-are-under-attack/

https://www.blackfacts.com/fact/ella-baker-1

The History of Queen Califia and the California Blacks By Qwest7, April 19, 2015https://eurweb.com/2015/04/19/the-history-of-queen-califia-and-the-california-blacks/

By Sola Rey, **Queen Gudit/Yodit of Ethiopia**, Africa, June 26, 2016, URL https://solarey.net/queen-gudit-ethiopia-africa/

By Jide Uwechia, Queen Khalifa (aka Califia/Calafia) **The Black Empress of California**, August 6, 2011, Don Jaide (Califia, Queen of California painting by Arthur Wright), https://www.africaresource.com/rasta/sesostris-the-great-the-egyptian-hercules/queen-khalifa-aka-califiacalafia-the-black-empress-of-california/comment-page-1/

By Thomas Brandstetter, **Women Combatants in the Haitian Revolution**, July 31, 2015, https://wargamingraft.wordpress.com/2015/07/31/women-combatants-in-the-haitian-revolution/ -Marie-Jeanne Lamartiniére, Suzanne Béliar Marie Sainte Dédée Bazile

By Ellen Lloyd -, **Amanirenas**, brave one-eyed Queen who defeated the ancient Romans, AncientPages.com, www.ancientpages.com/2019/01/30/amanirenas-brave-one-eyed-queen-of-kush-defeated-ancient-romans/

By Davie, L., (2012), **"Sara Baartman, at rest at last" From South Africa.Info**, May 14, Available at www.southafrica.info[Accessed: August 13, 2013], sahistory.org.za/people/sara-saartjie-baartman

ELOGEIA HADLEY

Billie Holiday Biography(1915–1959) UPDATED:JAN 12, 2021ORIGINAL:JAN 19, 2018https://www.biography.com/musician/billie-holiday

By Laura Etheredge, **Henrietta Lacks,** Encyclopedia Britannica, Encyclopedia Britannica, Inc. September 30, 2019, URL: https://www.britannica.com/biography/Henrietta-Lacks britannica.com/biography/**Henrietta-Lacks**

By Cameron Glover, Refinery29, **Who's Teaching Black Women About Financial Literacy?** April 10, 2017, yahoo.com/lifestyle/apos-teaching-black-women-financial-133000302.html

Black Past.com https://www.blackpast.org/global-african-history/baker-josephine-1906-1975/ JOSEPHINE BAKER (1906-1975), POSTED ON FEBRUARY 6, 2008 BY CONTRIBUTED BY: ZAKIYA ADAIR

By Jone Johnson Lewis, thoughco, **10 of the Most Important Black Women in U.S. History**, Updated November 16, 2019, thoughtco.com/notable-african-american-women-4151777

By Aderemi Ojekunle, Business Insider by PULSE, 09/09/2019 pulse.ng/bi/lifestyle/7-most-powerful-African-queens-in-history-you-need-to-know/dwhncf5, **Queen Nandi, Queen Yaa Asantewa, Queen Nefertiti, Princess Amina, Queen Sheba/Makeba**

By Leeza S. Haskell, Odyssey, **10 Black Women's Rights Activists Who Have Changed The Face Of Feminism, Angela Davis, Shirley Chisolm**, North Carolina Central University, February 9, 2017, theodysseyonline.com/10-black-womens-rights-activists-who-have-changed-the-face-of-feminism

By Erika Bryan, **Black Past.Com, Frances Cress Welsing** (1935–2016), March 19, 2016, https://www.blackpast.org/african-american-history/welsing-frances-cress-1935-2016/

By Biography.com Editors, **Nikki Giovanni Biography**, Publisher A&E Television Networks Last Updated, July 23, 2019, Original Published Date April 2, 2014, The Biography.com website https://www.biography.com/writer/nikki-giovanni

By Qwest7 **The History of Queen Califia and the California Blacks**, Published April 19, 2015, mobile.eurweb.com/2015/04/19/the-history-of-queen-califia-and-the-california-blacks/mobile.eurweb.com/2015/04/19/the-history-of-queen-califia-and-the-california-blacks/

By Peggy Epstein, **Famous Black Female Poets**, Updated February 21, 2017, https://penandthepad.com/famous-black-female-poets-5929633.html

By Merriam-Webster. (n.d.). **Self-respect**. In Merriam-Webster.com dictionary. Retrieved May 22, 2020, from https://www.merriam-webster.com/dictionary/self-respect

By Nnamdi Azikiwe, **How Much Is Melanin Worth In 2020**? Posted on January 2, 2020, https://keyamsha.com/2020/01/02/how-much-is-melanin-worth-in-2020/

By Dr.Laila O Afrika, Melanin: **What Makes Black People Black Paperback**, October 9, 2009, Holistic Therapies and Education Center, https://www.llailaafrika.com/product-category/books/

By **Dr. Joy DeGruy**, Post Traumatic Slave Syndrome, Posted on October 11, 2015, by Chief X, https://africanpeopleoflove.wordpress.com/2015/10/11/dr-joy-degruy/

By Nielsen, E. The black pas, **Mary Turner** (1899-1918), 2015, September 22 URLhttps://www.blackpast.org/african-american-history/mary-turner-1899-1918/age.com

By Celebages.com Tamika Mallory https://www.celebsages.com/tamika-mallory/

By Aderemi Ojekunle, **most powerful African queens in history you need to know**, September 9, 2019, https://www.pulse.ng/bi/lifestyle/7-most-powerful-african-queens-in-history-you-need-to-know/dwhncf5

By TheBlackList, afiong l afiong, **Affiong L. Affiong**, Pan Afrikan Lectures & Speaking Tour posted on November 8, 2011, https://www.theblacklist.net/profiles/blogs/affiong-l-affiong-pan-afrikan-lectures-amp-speaking-tour

By Cassidy Sparks, **The Budgetnista's Tifanny Aliche** gives recession-proof financial advice | May 29, 2020, https://rollingout.com/2020/05/29/the-budgetnista-tifanny-aliche-gives-financial-advice-for-recessions/ https://thebudgetnistablog.com/about-budgetnista-financial-help/

ELOGEIA HADLEY

By Akinwale Akinyoade, The Guardian life **Queen Moremi** Ajasoro: The Celebration of A Legendary Queen, May 31, 2019, https://guardian.ng/life/whatsnew/queen-moremi-ajasoro-the-celebration-of-a-legendary-queen/

By Publisher A&E, **Maya Angelou Biography**, Author Biography.com Editors, Updated January 31, 2020, Original Published Date, and April 2, 2014, Website Name The Biography.com website URL
https://www.biography.com/writer/maya-angelou

By Jae Jones, bulawayo1872.com, **Spiritualist Nehanda Charwe Nyakasikana**: "My Bones Will Rise Again" - Apr 24, 2020 - Black History, BLACK WOMEN, History, website
URLhttp://www.bulawayo1872.com/history/nehandambuya.htm

By Ricky Riley, Fearless Female Warriors: How the Great Kushite Ruler **Amanirenas** Brought Rome to Heel, October 21, 2016,
https://atlantablackstar.com/2016/10/21/fearless-female-warriors-how-the-great-kushite-ruler-amanirenas-brought-rome-to-heel/

By Ricky Riley, **Amanishakheto**, Warrior Queen of Nubia—6 Fascinating Facts You May Not Know, September 8, 2015, https://atlantablackstar.com/2015/09/08/amanishakheto-warrior-queen-of-nubia-6-fascinating-facts-you-may-not-know/3/

By Kimberly Wilson, **Protect Your Magic! 9 Self Care Acts Black Women Should Practice Daily**, September 24, 2018, https://www.essence.com/lifestyle/health-wellness/9-self-care-tips-black-women-should-practice-daily/

By Amy Marie Scott-Zerr, BlackPast, **Ahosi (Amazons) of Dahomey**, March 29, 2013, https://www.blackpast.org/global-african-history/groups-organizations-global-african-history/amazons-ahosi-dahomey/

By Ian Bernard, **Queen Nanny of the Maroons** (? – 1733), March 1, 2011, https://www.blackpast.org/global-african-history/queen-nanny-maroons-1733/

By Jessica Snethen, Blackpast, **Queen Nzinga** (1583-1663), June 16, 2009, https://www.blackpast.org/global-african-history/queen-nzinga-1583-1663/

ELOGEIA HADLEY

Meet the warrior woman from Dahomey who trained Haitian revolutionary hero Dessalines

By Elizabeth Ofosuah Johnson, **Adbaraya Toya**-Meet the warrior woman from Dahomey who trained Haitian revolutionary hero Dessalines, March 12, 2019, https://face2faceafrica.com/article/meet-the-warrior-woman-from-dahomey-who-trained-haitian-revolutionary-hero-dessalines

By Elizabeth Ofosuah Johnson, The story of **Breffu**, a female slave from Ghana who led a massive slave revolt to take over the west indies, September 3, 2018, https://face2faceafrica.com/article/the-story-of-breffu-a-female-slave-from-ghana-who-led-a-massive-slave-revolt-to-take-over-the-west-indies-in-1733

By: John Mason, Arab America, Arab America Contributing Writer An Early Feminist: **Al-Kahina**, 7th Century North African Queen--Fact or Fancy? Posted, October 31, 2018, https://www.arabamerica.com/an-early-feminist-al-kahina-7th-century-north-african-queen-fact-or-fancy/

by Meserette Kentake, **The Hanging of Celia** December 21, 2015, https://kentakepage.com/the-hanging-of-celia/

By sola rey African Princess: **Yennenga the Svelte of Burkina Faso**, Jan 4, 2018, African Princess: Yennenga the Svelte of Burkina Faso, http://solarey.net/tag/female-warriors/

By Shirley Yee, BlackPast, **Harriet Ross Tubman** (ca. 1821-1913), February 11, 2007, https://www.blackpast.org/african-american-history/tubman-harriet-ross-c-1821-1913/

By Ian Bernard, BlackPast, **Queen Nanny of the Maroons (? – 1733)**, March 1, 2011, https://www.blackpast.org/global-african-history/queen-nanny-maroons-1733/

By Brad Smithfield, The legend of the martyred **St. Escrava Anastacia**, the beautiful slave girl who was forced to wear a face mask, March 14, 2017, https://www.thevintagenews.com/2017/03/14/the-legend-of-the-martyred-st-escrava-anastacia-the-beautiful-slave-girl-who-was-forced-to-wear-a-face-mask/

ELOGEIA HADLEY

By Euell A. Nielsen, BlackPast, **Carlotta Lucumi**, "La Negra Carlota" (?- 1844), May 9, 2020, https://www.blackpast.org/global-african-history/carlotta-lucumi-la-negra-carlota-1844/

By Priscilla Pope-Levison, BlackPast**, Sojourner Truth (ca. 1791-1883)**, January 21, 2007, https://www.blackpast.org/african-american-history/truth-sojourner-isabella-baumfree-ca-1791-1883/

By BlackPast, BlackPast (1909) **Ida B. Wells**, "Lynching, Our National Crime" September 22, 2008, https://www.blackpast.org/african-american-history/1909-ida-b-wells-awful-slaughter/

By Sarah Bartlett, BlackPast, **Winnie Madikizela-Mandela (1936-2018)**, October 4, 2010, contributed https://www.blackpast.org/global-african-history/mandela-winnie-madikizela-1936/

By Samuel Momodu, BlackPast, **Ava Marie DuVernay** (1972-), August 15, 2016, https://www.blackpast.org/african-american-history/duvernay-ava-marie-1972/

By Catherine Foster, BlackPast, **Oprah Winfrey (1954-),** February 3, 2007, https://www.blackpast.org/african-american-history/winfrey-oprah-1954/

By Farida Dawkins, BlackPast, **Tignon Laws: The dreadful rule that banned black women from displaying their hair**, February 5, 2018, https://face2faceafrica.com/article/tignon-laws-the-dreadful-rule-that-banned-black-women-from-displaying-their-hair

By Prouty, Chris, **Empress Taytu and Menilek II**: Ethiopia 1883-1910. Schwarz-Bart, Simone. In Praise of Black Women Volume 2: Heroines of the Slavery Era. "Taytu Betul: the Rise of an Itege." Unesco. <http://unesdoc.unesco.org/images/0023/002331/233138E.pdf>

By Farida Dawkins, face2faceafrica, **The untold story of the great Nubian Queen Shanakdakhete who ruled without a king**, July 10, 2018, https://face2faceafrica.com/article/the-untold-story-of-the-great-nubian-queen-shanakdakhete-who-ruled-without-a-king

ELOGEIA HADLEY

By Sean Liburd **Queen Afua**: We Celebrate Your Healing Wisdom March 15, 2018, https://seanliburd.com/2018/03/15/queen-afua-we-celebrate-your-healing-wisdom/

By Jone Johnson Lewis, **Hatshepsut**: She Became a Female Pharaoh of Egypt, How Did She Become a Pharaoh in Ancient Egypt?, Updated January 12, 2018, https://www.thoughtco.com/hatshepsut-biography-3524878

By David Tee - AncientPages.com, Life, And Legacy Of **Queen Tiye**, Mother Of Akhenaten – Was She Egyptian Or Nubian?Last Updated on March 16, 2019, http://www.ancientpages.com/2018/07/20/life-queen-tiye-mother-of-akhenaten-was-she-egyptian-or-nubian/

By Epiphany's Spectrums Of Ebony at, **La Mulâtresse Solitude**, April 26, 2017, https://ourunsungstory.blogspot.com/2017/04/la-mulatresse-solitude.html

By Vicki Maikutena Matson-Green, **Tarenorerer** (1800–1831) Australian Dictionary of Biographyhttp://adb.anu.edu.au/biography/tarenorerer-13212

By Priscilla Q. Williams, RN- Author, Speaker, Certified Life Coach, **Global Nurse Educator Black Women And The Truth About Mental Health**, December 27, 2018, http://www.priscillaqwilliams.com

By Marquita K. Harris, **33 Successful Black Women Who'll Inspire You To Chase Your Dreams,** May 22, 2020, https://www.essence.com/news/money-career/entrepreneurship/25-black-women-entrepreneurs/

By Jonathan P. Hicks, **Poll: Black Women Most Religious Group in America, black women are among the most religious demographic group in the country, according to a survey**. Published July 9, 2012, https://www.bet.com/news/national/2012/07/09/poll-black-women-most-religious-group-in-america.html

By Rochaun Meadows-Fernandez — **Strong Black Women Are Allowed to Have Depression, Too,** April 18, 2018,https://www.healthline.com/health/black-women-are-allowed-to-have-depression-too#1

By Theodora Aidoo, Face2Face, Did you know there are only three black female billionaires in the world?

ELOGEIA HADLEY

November 13, 2019, https://face2faceafrica.com/article/did-you-know-there-are-only-three-black-female-billionaires-in-the-world **Oprah Winfrey, Folorunsho Alakija, and Isabel Dos Santos**

By Madamenoire, Madamenoire, December 30, 2011, **are black mothers failing to raise their sons**, https://madamenoire.com/122785/are-black-mothers-failing-to-raise-their-sons/

By The editors of Encyclopedia Britannica, Encyclopedia Britannica, **Fannie Lou Hamer**, March 10, 2020, URL:https://www.britannica.com/biography/Fannie-Lou-Hamer-American-civil-rights-activist

By Michael Harriot, The Root, The Myth of the **'Angry Black Woman'** and Advertising's Fight to End It, 9/27/17, https://thegrapevine.theroot.com/the-myth-of-the-angry-black-woman-and-advertisings-fig-1818840794

by Tamara Winfrey Harris / Bitch Magazine, AlterNet, The Truth Behind the **"Strong Black Woman"** Stereotype, November 6, 2014, https://www.alternet.org/2014/11/truth-behind-strong-black-woman-stereotype/

By Tana Gilmore, The Matchmaking DUO Top 7 Reasons **Why Single Black Men Don't Approach Black Women**, February 17, 2015, https://www.essence.com/love/relationships/top-7-reasons-why-single-black-men-dont-approach-black-women/#153923

By Genefe Navilon, HackSpirit**, Emotional baggage**: 6 signs you have it and how to let it go, January 2, 2020, https://hackspirit.com/emotional-baggage-signs-you-have-it-and-how-to-let-it-go/

The Patriot,Origins of the 'Moor' **Nugaymath amazon warriror** By admin -September 26, 2019https://www.thepatriot.co.zw/old_posts/origins-of-the-moor/

By OBWS Official Black Wall Street, **Team Black, the Race Riot That Destroyed Black Wall Street**, July 22, 2015, https://officialblackwallstreet.com/black-wall-street-story/

BY, The Editors of Encyclopaedia **Carol Moseley Braun,** Britannicahttps://www.britannica.com/biography/Carol-Moseley-Braun

ELOGEIA HADLEY

By Michael Taylor **the tale of" No Name"** Thu 23 Jul
2020 02.30 EDT Last modified on Tue 22 Sep 2020 03.32,
Murder on the Middle Passage by Nicholas Rogers review
– slavery and the British empire
https://www.theguardian.com/books/2020/jul/23/on-the-
middle-passage-by-nicholas-rogers-review-slavery-and-the-
british-empire

 Biography, **Ruby Bridges**
https://www.biography.com/activist/ruby-
bridgesUPDATED:JUN 22, 2020ORIGINAL: APR 27,
2017

**64,000 African-American Women Currently Missing In
The U.S.** by Shantia Brown,
https://www.storyhulk.com/2019/11/29/64000-african-
american/

AUDLEY MOORE (1898-1997)Queen Mother Moore
POSTED ON JUNE 6, 2011BY CONTRIBUTED BY:
DWAYNE MACK, Black and missing foundation,
http://www.blackandmissinginc.com/cdad/

**#SayHerName: Black Women And Girls Killed By
Police**, Posted May 12, 2020, Written By NewsOne Staff,

Posted May 12, 2020https://www.blackpast.org/african-american-history/moore-audley-1898-1997/

Raising Black Children in a Racist Society, SEPTEMBER 10, 2020|IN RELATIONSHIPS/FAMILY, CURRENT EVENTS, CHRISTIAN LIVING|BY JOEL A. BOWMAN SR. https://thewitnessbcc.com/raising-black-children-in-a-racist-society/

Sister Souljah's long-awaited sequel to 'The Coldest Winter Ever' to be published by Atria in March By KARU F. DANIELS, NEW YORK DAILY NEWS DEC 04, 2020 AT 9:13 PMhttps://www.nydailynews.com/snyde/ny-sister-souljah-coldest-winter-ever-sequel-atria-release-march-2021-20201205-vu7bax5hffcibcnlkx4w6bisdy-story.html

Empress Zewditu of Ethiopia, Africa, May 3, 2016, 0 CommentsWritten by sola Rey, http://solarey.net/empress-zewditu/

BLACK PAST, **DOROTHY COUNTS** (1942-)POSTED ON AUGUST 31, 2016 BY CONTRIBUTED BY: SAMUEL MOMODU, https://www.blackpast.org/african-american-history/counts-dorothy-1942/

ELOGEIA HADLEY

By IBW21October 1, **2020 Dr. Patricia a Newton Dr. Patricia Newton**, Rest in power tribute, Black Family Summit News, News & Current Affairs

By zimbio. Com, **marsi martin,** https://www.zimbio.com/photos/Marsai+Martin/piRPvUex 0Ul/24th+Annual+Screen+Actors+Guild+Awards+Arrivals

By Laura Rahme's, **Aline Sitoe,** Teranga, and sun, http://teranga-and-sun.blogspot.com/2014/02/aline-sitoe-diatta-joan-of-arc-of-africa.html

By Jennifer Harlan and Giulia McDonnell Nieto del Rio, Bethany Mollenkopf, Imani Khayyam, Lawrence Agyei, Akilah Townsend, Liam Woods, Anissa Baty for New York Times, **A Record Number of Black Women Run Some of the Biggest U.S. Cities Black women achieved a historic milestone as mayors of eight major American cities this year.** Political analysts say the record number points to "the age of Black women in politics." Published Oct. 27, 2021, Updated Nov. 3, 2021https://www.nytimes.com/2021/10/27/us/black-women-mayor-us-cities.html

Pictures by Google images and from the previous links and sites

DEFINITIONS

The code switch - In a white world, code-switching is a necessary adaption for black people. Code-switching is the process of shifting from one linguistic code to another, depending on the social or conversational setting. For black people, this means having the ability to switch from

AAVE *(AAVE)*-African American Vernacular English to "proper English" whenever it is deemed appropriate.

Kemet or 'km.t' is the name of Ancient Egyptian prior Greeks occupation, it translates to the "black land" or "the land of the blacks" or the land of the black soil, but Kemet means black people Kemet/'km.t'.

KandakeQueen or Queen mother

This book is for and not limited to educational purposes

" Protect your peace at all costs. Anything that disturbs your peace is too expensive."

– Malanda Jean Claude

ABOUT THE AUTHOR

ELOGEIA HADLEY

WHO IS SHE?

Born in Chicago, Illinois, Elogeia Hadley was raised by her love parents, Julius and Faye Carter. Hadley is the oldest of four siblings; one brother and two sisters, and she, too, grew up to marry and now has four children of her own; two boys and two girls.

Research and writing have always been a taste of enjoyment for Hadley. She not only has two books (*are they research books or thrillers*) that precede this one, titled X and X, but she also continues to thrive and has two more projects in the making.

Hadley has a personal desire to give back to the community that surrounds her. She has started a club called *divasNdaughters* for females and family friends, where once a year, they get together and support one another. To add to Hadley's expressiveness, she has a store on Etsy called "*knowURGreat*," where she sells pride t-shirts. Ultimately, Hadley's passion is to empower our children and build bonds between our families. She truly has a heart of gold.

ELOGEIA HADLEY

*9 7 8 1 9 5 3 1 6 3 4 9 3 *